PHP
Pocket Reference

SECOND EDITION

PHP
Pocket Reference

Rasmus Lerdorf

O'REILLY®

Beijing · Cambridge · Farnham · Köln · Paris · Sebastopol · Taipei · Tokyo

PHP Pocket Reference, Second Edition

by Rasmus Lerdorf

Published by O'Reilly Media, Inc., 1005 Gravenstein Highway North,
Sebastopol, CA 95472.

O'Reilly Media, Inc. books may be purchased for educational,
business, or sales promotional use. Online editions are also available
for most titles (*safari.oreilly.com*). For more information, contact our
corporate/institutional sales department: (800) 998-9938 or
corporate@oreilly.com.

Editor:	Paula Ferguson
Production Editor:	Colleen Gorman
Cover Designer:	Ellie Volckhausen
Interior Designer:	David Futato

Printing History:

January 2000:	First Edition
November 2002:	Second Edition

0-596-00402-8
[C]   [6/04]

Contents

PHP Pocket Reference

Introduction

PHP (PHP Hypertext Preprocessor) is a web scripting language. It was specifically designed to solve "the web problem." PHP is easy to learn because it builds on the bits and pieces that most people already know. The pieces that you don't know are filled in by excellent online documentation and many high-quality books. This simple approach to solving the web problem has caught on with an amazing number of people.

This pocket reference further simplifies things by focusing on the absolute essentials. It provides an overview of the main concepts needed for most web applications, followed by quick reference material for most of the main PHP functions.

Installation and Configuration

PHP works with many different web servers in many different ways, but by far the most popular way to run PHP is as an Apache module with Apache 1.3.x. Full installation instructions for all the different ways to install PHP can be found in the PHP documentation. Here, I cover the Apache module installation.

If you are compiling from the PHP source tarball, follow the instructions in the *INSTALL* file found inside the PHP distribution file. A tarball is a compressed *tar* file. *tar* stands for tape archive, but these days it has little to do with tapes. It is simply a way to lump multiple files and directories into a single file for distribution. Normally tarballs have the *.tar.gz* extension to indicate a *tar* file compressed with *gzip*. To untar a tarball, use:

```
tar zxvf foo.tar.gz
```

On Windows, many utilities (including WinZip) understand tarballs.

If you are installing from a precompiled binary package such as an *rpm* file, most of the work should be done for you. But doublecheck that the Apache configuration described below is correct.

When you are using PHP as an Apache module, PHP processing is triggered by a special MIME type. This is defined in the Apache configuration file with a line similar to:

```
AddType application/x-httpd-php .php
```

This line tells Apache to treat all files that end with the *.php* extension as PHP files, which means that any file with that extension is parsed for PHP tags. The actual extension is completely arbitrary and you are free to change it to whatever you wish to use.

If you are running PHP as a dynamic shared object (DSO) module, you also need this line in your Apache configuration file:

```
LoadModule php4_module    modules/libphp4.so
```

Note that in many default *httpd.conf* files you will find AddModule lines. These really aren't necessary. They are only needed if you have a ClearModuleList directive somewhere in your *httpd.conf* file. I would suggest simply deleting the ClearModuleList directive and deleting all your AddModule lines. The idea behind ClearModuleList/AddModule is to make it possible to reorder already loaded modules in case module order is an issue. With most modules, the order that they are loaded—which governs the order they are called—is not important. And further, most binary distributions of Apache ship with most modules compiled as dynamically loadable modules, which means that if order is an issue for some reason, you can simply change the order of the LoadModule calls to fix it.

Don't forget to restart your server after making changes to your *httpd.conf* file. Once the server is restarted, you can check to see if PHP is working by creating a file in your document root named *info.php* containing the single line:

```
<?php phpinfo()?>
```

Load this up in your browser using *http://your.domain.com/info.php*. You should see all sorts of information about PHP. If you don't see anything, try selecting "View Source" in your browser. If you see the phpinfo() line, you probably forgot (or mistyped) the AddType line in your *httpd.conf* file. If the browser tries to download the file instead, it means that the AddType is there, but the PHP module is not being triggered—perhaps because you forgot the LoadModule line.

Once you have verified that PHP is working, have a look at the PHP initialization file called *php.ini*. The phpinfo() page will tell you where PHP is expecting to find it. PHP functions fine without this file, but with all the default settings. If you want to change the defaults, or perhaps more importantly, you want to be immune from any changes to the defaults when you upgrade, you should create a *php.ini* file. The source distribution of PHP comes with a *php.ini-dist* file that you can rename and copy into the location specified in the phpinfo() output. The *php.ini* file itself is well-commented and self-explanatory for the most part.

You can also put configuration directives inside the Apache *httpd.conf* file, and, in certain cases, in individual *.htaccess* files. This is very useful for setting things per-directory or per-virtual host. If you have this line in the *php.ini* file:

```
include_path = ".:/usr/local/lib/php:.."
```

you can set this in your *httpd.conf* file with:

```
php_value include_path .:/usr/local/lib/php:..
```

There are four *httpd.conf* directives used for setting PHP directives:

php_value
> For setting normal strings and values

php_flag
> For setting boolean values

php_admin_value
> For setting administrative values

php_admin_flag
> For setting boolean administrative values.

In addition, the normal values and booleans can be set in your *.htaccess* files, but only if the Apache AllowOverride setting (which sets what is allowed in a *.htaccess* file) includes "Options".

More information can be found at *http://www.php.net/configuration*.

Embedding PHP in HTML

You embed PHP code into a standard HTML page. For example, here's how you can dynamically generate the title of an HTML document:

```
<html><head><title><?echo $title?></title>
</head>...
```

The <?echo $title?> portion of the document is replaced by the contents of the $title PHP variable. echo is a basic language statement that you can use to output data.

There are a few different ways to embed your PHP code. As you just saw, you can put PHP code between <? and ?> tags:

```
<? echo "Hello World"; ?>
```

This style is the most common way to embed PHP, but it is a problem if your PHP code needs to co-exist with XML, as XML may use that tagging style itself. If this is the case, turn off this style in the *php.ini* file with the short_open_tag directive. Another way to embed PHP code is within <?php and ?> tags:

```
<?php echo "Hello World"; ?>
```

This style is always available and is recommended when your PHP code needs to be portable to many different systems. Embedding PHP within <script> tags is another style that is always available:

```
<script language="php" > echo "Hello World";
</script>
```

One final style, in which the code is between <% and %> tags, is disabled by default:

```
<% echo "Hello World"; %>
```

You can turn on this style with the asp_tags directive in your *php.ini* file. The style is most useful when you are using Microsoft FrontPage or another HTML authoring tool that prefers that tag style for HTML-embedded scripts.

You can embed multiple statements by separating them with semicolons:

```
<?php
  echo "Hello World";
  echo "A second statement";
?>
```

It is legal to switch back and forth between HTML and PHP at any time. For example, if you want to output 100 <br /> tags for some reason, you can do it this way:

```
<?php for($i=0; $i<100; $i++) { ?>
  <br />
<?php } ?>
```

Of course, using the str_repeat() function here would make more sense.

When you embed PHP code in an HTML file, you need to use the *.php* file extension for that file, so that your web server knows to send the file to PHP for processing. Or, if you have configured your web server to use a different extension for PHP files, use that extension instead.

When you have PHP code embedded in an HTML page, you can think of that page as a PHP program. The bits and pieces of HTML and PHP combine to provide the functionality of the program. A collection of pages that contain programs can be thought of as a web application.

Including Files

An important feature of PHP is its ability to include files. These files may contain additional PHP tags. When you are designing a web application, you can break out common components and place them in a single file. This step makes it much easier to change certain aspects in one place later, and have the change take effect across the entire application. To include a file, use the include keyword:

```
<?php
    $title="My Cool Web Application";
    include "header.inc";
?>
```

The *header.inc* file might look as follows:

```
<html><head>
<title><?php echo $title?></title>
</head>
```

This example illustrates two important concepts of included files in PHP. First, variables set in the including file are automatically available in the included file. Second, each included file starts out in HTML mode. In other words, if you want to include a file that has PHP code in it, you have to embed that code just as you would any other PHP code.

Note also that I used the *.inc* extension here. This is not a special file type, just an arbitrary extension name I chose. Since your Apache server is not set up to treat *.inc* files as PHP files, if you put this file somewhere under your document_root, people can browse to it and see the PHP source in that file directly. This is usually not a good idea, so I add these lines to my *httpd.conf* file:

```
<Files ~ "\.inc$">
   Order allow,deny
   Deny from all
</Files>
```

This blocks any direct access to *.inc* files.

The other option is to not put the files under document_root, or perhaps to name them *.php* instead. But be very careful with that last approach. Keep in mind that people will then be able to execute these scripts, when they were probably not designed to be executed in a standalone fashion.

Other ways to include files are through include_once, require, and require_once. The difference between include and require is simply that with include, if the file to be included does not exist, you get a warning, whereas with require you get a fatal error and script execution stops. The include_once and require_once variations ensure that the file being included has not been included already. This helps avoid things like function redefinition errors.

Language Syntax

Variable names in PHP are case-sensitive. That means $A and $a are two distinct variables. However, function names in PHP are not case-sensitive. This rule applies to both built-in functions and user-defined functions.

PHP ignores whitespace between tokens. You can use spaces, tabs, and newlines to format and indent your code to make it more readable. PHP statements are terminated by semicolons.

There are three types of comments in PHP:

```
/* C style comments */
// C++ style comments
# Bourne shell style comments
```

The C++ and Bourne shell–style comments can be inserted anywhere in your code. Everything from the comment characters to the end of the line is ignored. The C-style comment tells PHP to ignore everything from the start of the comment until the end-comment characters. This means that this style of comment can span multiple lines.

Variables

In PHP, all variable names begin with a dollar sign ($). The $ is followed by an alphabetic character or an underscore, and optionally followed by a sequence of alphanumeric characters and underscores. There is no limit on the length of a variable name. Variable names in PHP are case-sensitive. Here are some examples:

```
$i
$counter
$first_name
$_TMP
```

In PHP, unlike in many other languages, you do not have to explicitly declare variables. PHP automatically declares a variable the first time a value is assigned to it. PHP variables are untyped; you can assign a value of any type to a variable.

PHP uses a symbol table to store the list of variable names and their values. There are two kinds of symbol tables in PHP: the global symbol table, which stores the list of global variables, and the function-local symbol table, which stores the set of variables available inside each function.

Dynamic Variables

Sometimes it is useful to set and use variables dynamically. Normally, you assign a variable like this:

```
$var = "hello";
```

Now let's say you want a variable whose name is the value of the $var variable. You can do that like this:

```
$$var = "World";
```

PHP parses $$var by first dereferencing the innermost variable, meaning that $var becomes "hello". The expression that's left is $"hello", which is just $hello. In other words, we have just created a new variable named hello and assigned it the value "World". You can nest dynamic variables to an infinite level in PHP, although once you get beyond two levels, it can be very confusing for someone who is trying to read your code.

There is a special syntax for using dynamic variables, and any other complex variable, inside quoted strings in PHP:

```
echo "Hello ${$var}";
```

This syntax also helps resolve an ambiguity that occurs when variable arrays are used. Something like $$var[1] is ambiguous because it is impossible for PHP to know which level to apply the array index to. ${$var[1]} tells PHP to dereference the inner level first and apply the array index to the result before dereferencing the outer level. ${$var}[1], on the other hand, tells PHP to apply the index to the outer level.

Initially, dynamic variables may not seem that useful, but there are times when they can shorten the amount of code you need to write to perform certain tasks. For example, say you have an associative array that looks like:

```
$array["abc"] = "Hello";
$array["def"] = "World";
```

Associative arrays like this are returned by various functions in the PHP modules. `mysql_fetch_array()` is one example. The indices in the array usually refer to fields or entity names within the context of the module you are working with. It's handy to turn these entity names into real PHP variables, so you can refer to them as simply $abc and $def. This is done as follows:

```
foreach($array as $index=>$value) {
  $$index = $value;
}
```

Data Types

PHP provides four primitive data types: integers, floating point numbers, strings, and booleans. In addition, there are two compound data types: arrays and objects.

Integers

Integers are whole numbers. The range of integers in PHP is equivalent to the range of the long data type in C. On 32-bit platforms, integer values range from −2,147,483,648 to +2,147,483,647. PHP automatically converts larger values to floating point numbers if you happen to overflow the range. An integer can be expressed in decimal (base-10), hexadecimal (base-16), or octal (base-8). For example:

```
$decimal=16;
$hex=0x10;
$octal=020;
```

Floating Point Numbers

Floating point numbers represent decimal values. The range of floating point numbers in PHP is equivalent to the range of the double type in C. On most platforms, a double can be between 1.7E–308 to 1.7E+308. A double may be expressed either as a regular number with a decimal point or in scientific notation. For example:

```
$var=0.017;
$var=17.0E-3
```

PHP also has two sets of functions that let you manipulate numbers with arbitrary precision. These two sets are known as the BC and the GMP functions. See *http://www.php.net/bc* and *http://www.php.net/gmp* for more information.

Strings

A string is a sequence of characters. A string can be delimited by single quotes or double quotes:

```
'PHP is cool'
"Hello, World!"
```

Double-quoted strings are subject to variable substitution and escape sequence handling, while single quotes are not. For example:

```
$a="World";
echo "Hello\t$a\n";
```

This displays "Hello" followed by a tab and then "World" followed by a newline. In other words, variable substitution is performed on the variable $a and the escape sequences are converted to their corresponding characters. Contrast that with:

```
echo 'Hello\t$a\n';
```

In this case, the output is exactly "Hello\t$a\n". There is no variable substitution or handling of escape sequences.

Another way to assign a string is to use what is known as the *heredoc* syntax. The advantage with this approach is that you do not need to escape quotes. It looks like this:

```
$foo = <<<EOD
  This is a "multiline" string
  assigned using the 'heredoc' syntax.
EOD;
```

The following table shows the escape sequences understood by PHP inside double-quoted strings.

Escape sequence	Meaning
\n	Linefeed (LF or 0x0A (10) in ASCII)
\r	Carriage return (CR or 0x0D (13) in ASCII)
\t	Horizontal tab (HT or 0x09 (9) in ASCII)
\\	Backslash
\$	Dollar sign
\"	Double quote
\123	Octal notation representation of a character
\x12	Hexadecimal notation representation of a character

Booleans

The boolean type only has two states: true and false. For example:

```
$flag = true;
```

Boolean values are most commonly used when the == or === operators perform a comparison and return the result.

Arrays

An array is a compound data type that can contain multiple data values, indexed either numerically or with strings. For example, an array of strings can be written like this:

```
$var[0]="Hello";
$var[1]="World";
```

Note that when you assign array elements like this, you do not have to use consecutive numbers to index the elements.

As a shortcut, PHP allows you to add an element onto the end of an array without specifying an index. For example:

```
$var[] ="Test";
```

PHP picks the next logical numerical index. In this case, the "Test" element is given the index 2 in our $var array: if the array has nonconsecutive elements, PHP selects the index value that is one greater than the current highest index value. This autoindexing feature is most useful when dealing with multiple-choice HTML <select> form elements, as we'll see in a later example.

Although we have called strings a primitive data type, it is actually possible to treat a string as a compound data type, where each character in the string can be accessed separately. In other words, you can think of a string as an array of characters, where the first character is at index 0. Thus, you can pick the third character out of a string with:

```
$string[2]
```

To solve an ambiguity problem between strings and arrays, a new syntax has been introduced to dereference individual characters from strings:

```
$string{2}
```

This syntax is equivalent to $string[2], and is preferable.

Arrays can also be indexed using strings; these kinds of arrays are called *associative arrays*:

```
$var["January"]=1;
$var["February"]=2;
```

You can use a mix of numerical and string indices with a single array because PHP treats all arrays as hash tables internally, and the hash, or index, can be whatever you want.

All arrays in PHP can be traversed safely with the following mechanism:

```
foreach($array as $key=>$value) {
  echo "array[$key]=$value<br>\n";
}
```

This is the most common way to loop through each element of an array, whether it is a linear or an associative array. PHP provides a number of array manipulation functions; these are detailed later in the "Function Reference."

Objects

An object is a compound data type that can contain any number of variables and functions. PHP's support for objects is somewhat limited in Version 4. PHP Version 5 will improve the object-oriented capabilities of PHP. In PHP 4, the object-oriented support is designed to make it easy to encapsulate data structures and functions in order to package them into reusable classes. Here's a simple example:

```
class test {
  var $str = "Hello World";
  function init($str) {
    $this->str = $str;
  }
}

$class = new test;
echo $class->str;
$class->init("Hello");
echo $class->str;
```

This code creates a test object using the new operator. Then it sets a variable called str within the object. In object-speak, a variable in an object is known as a property of that object. The test object also defines a function, known as a method, called init(). This method uses the special-purpose $this variable to change the value of the str property within that object.

Inheritance is supported by using the extends keyword in the class definition. We can extend the previous test class like this:

```
class more extends test {
  function more() {
    echo "Constructor called";
  }
}
```

This means that the more class inherits from the test class and it also introduces the concept of a constructor. If a method inside a class has the same name as the class, it becomes the constructor function for that class. A constructor is called automatically when the class is instantiated.

Much more information is available at *http://www.php.net/oop*.

Type Casting

As I already mentioned, you do not need to specify a type when you create a variable, but that doesn't mean the variables do not have types associated with them. You can explicitly set the type, known as type casting, by using the C-style syntax in which you put the type you want in brackets before the variable or expression. For example:

```
$var = (int)"123abc";
```

Without the (int) in this example, PHP creates a string variable. With the explicit cast, however, we have created an integer variable with a value of 123. The following table shows the available cast operators in PHP.

Operators	Function
(int), (integer)	Cast to an integer
(real), (double), (float)	Cash to a floating point number
(string)	Cast to a string
(array)	Cast to an array
(object)	Cast to an object
(bool), (boolean)	Cast to a boolean
(unset)	Cast to NULL; the same as calling unset() on the value

Although they are not usually needed, PHP does provide the following built-in functions to check variable types in your program: gettype(), is_bool(), is_long(), is_float(), is_string(), is_array(), and is_object().

Expressions

An expression is the basic building block of the language. Anything with a value can be thought of as an expression. Examples include:

```
5
5+5
$a
$a==5
sqrt(9)
```

By combining many of these basic expressions, you can build larger, more complex expressions.

Note that the echo statement we've used in numerous examples cannot be part of a complex expression because it does not have a return value. The print statement, on the other hand, can be used as part of complex expression—it does have a return value. In all other respects, echo and print are identical: they output data.

Operators

Expressions are combined and manipulated using operators. The following table lists the operators from highest to lowest precedence; the second column (A) shows the operators' associativity. These operators should be familiar to you if you have any C, Java, or Perl experience.

Operators	A
!, ~, ++, --, @, (the casting operators)	Right
*, /, %	Left
+, -, .	Left
<<, >>	Left
<, <=, >=, >	Nonassociative
==, !=, ===, !==	Nonassociative

Operators	A
&	Left
^	Left
|	Left
&&	Left
||	Left
? : (conditional operator)	Left
=, +=, -=, *=, /=, %=, ^=, .=, &=, |=, <<=, >>=	Left
AND	Left
XOR	Left
OR	Left

Control Structures

The control structures in PHP are very similar to those used by the C language. Control structures are used to control the logical flow through a PHP script. PHP's control structures have two syntaxes that can be used interchangeably. The first form uses C-style curly braces to enclose statement blocks, while the second style uses a more verbose syntax that includes explicit ending statements. The first style is preferable when the control structure is completely within a PHP code block. The second style is useful when the construct spans a large section of intermixed code and HTML. The two styles are completely interchangeable, however, so it is really a matter of personal preference which one you use.

if

The if statement is a standard conditional found in most languages. Here are the two syntaxes for the if statement:

```
if(expr) {              if(expr):
    statements              statements
} elseif(expr) {        elseif(expr):
    statements              statements
```

```
} else {                else:
   statements              statements
}                       endif;
```

The if statement causes particular code to be executed if the expression it acts on is true. With the first form, you can omit the braces if you only need to execute a single statement.

switch

The switch statement can be used in place of a lengthy if statement. Here are the two syntaxes for switch:

```
switch(expr) {          switch(expr):
   case expr:              case expr:
      statements              statements
      break;                  break;
   default:                default:
      statements              statements
      break;                  break;
}                       endswitch;
```

The expression for each case statement is compared against the switch expression and, if they match, the code following that particular case is executed. The break keyword signals the end of a particular case; it may be omitted, which causes control to flow into the next case. If none of the case expressions match the switch expression, the default case is executed.

while

The while statement is a looping construct that repeatedly executes some code while a particular expression is true:

```
while(expr) {           while(expr):
   statements              statements
}                       endwhile;
```

The while expression is checked before the start of each iteration. If the expression evaluates to true, the code within the loop is executed. If the expression evaluates to false, however, execution skips to the code immediately following the while loop. Note that you can omit the curly braces with the first form of the while statement if you only need to execute a single statement.

It is possible to break out of a running loop at any time using the break keyword. This stops the current loop and, if control is within a nested set of loops, the next outer loop continues. It is also possible to break out of many levels of nested loops by passing a numerical argument to the break statement (break *n*) that specifies the number of nested loops it should break out of. You can skip the rest of a given loop and go onto the next iteration by using the continue keyword. With continue *n*, you can skip the current iterations of the *n* innermost loops.

do/while

The do/while statement is similar to the while statement, except that the conditional expression is checked at the end of each iteration instead of before:

```
do {
    statements
} while(expr);
```

Note that due to the order of the parts of this statement, there is only one valid syntax. If you only need to execute a single statement, you can omit the curly braces from the syntax. The break and continue statements work with this statement in the same way that they do with the while statement.

for

A for loop is a more complex looping construct than the simple while loop:

```
for(start_expr; cond_expr; iter_expr) {
    statements
}

for(start_expr; cond_expr; iter_expr):
    statements
endfor;
```

A for loop takes three expressions. The first is the start expression; it is evaluated once when the loop begins. This is generally used for initializing a loop counter. The second expression is a conditional expression that controls the iteration of the loop. This expression is checked prior to each iteration. The third expression, the iterative expression, is evaluated at the end of each iteration and is typically used to increment the loop counter. With the first form of the for statement, you can omit the braces if you only need to execute a single statement.

The break and continue statements work with a for loop like they do with a while loop, except that continue causes the iterative expression to be evaluated before the loop conditional expression is checked.

foreach

A foreach loop is used to loop through an array. Here are both forms of the syntax:

```
foreach(array_expression as $value) {
  statements
}

foreach(array_expression as $value):
  statements
endforeach;
```

This loops through the *array_expression* and assigns each value of the array to $value in turn. You can also get the key for each element with this syntax:

```
foreach(array_expression as $key=>$value) {
  statements
}
```

The break and continue statements work with a foreach loop like they do with a for loop.

Functions

A function is a named sequence of code statements that can optionally accept parameters and return a value. A function call is an expression that has a value; its value is the returned value from the function. PHP provides a large number of internal functions. The "Function Reference" section lists all of the commonly available functions. PHP also supports user-definable functions. To define a function, use the function keyword. For example:

```
function soundcheck($a, $b, $c) {
  return "Testing, $a, $b, $c";
}
```

When you define a function, be careful what name you give it. In particular, you need to make sure that the name does not conflict with any of the internal PHP functions. If you do use a function name that conflicts with an internal function, you get the following error:

```
Fatal error: Can't redeclare already declared function in
filename on line N
```

After you define a function, you call it by passing in the appropriate arguments. For example:

```
echo soundcheck(4, 5, 6);
```

You can also create functions with optional parameters. To do so, you set a default value for each optional parameter in the definition, using C++ style. For example, here's how to make all the parameters to the soundcheck() function optional:

```
function soundcheck($a=1, $b=2, $c=3) {
  return "Testing, $a, $b, $c";
}
```

Passing Arguments to Functions

There are two ways you can pass arguments to a function: by value and by reference. To pass an argument by value, you pass in any valid expression. That expression is evaluated and the value is assigned to the corresponding parameter defined within the function. Any changes you make to the parameter within the function have no effect on the argument passed to the function. For example:

```
function triple($x) {
  $x=$x*3;
  return $x;
}
$var=10;
$triplevar=triple($var);
```

In this case, $var evaluates to 10 when triple() is called, so $x is set to 10 inside the function. When $x is tripled, that change does not affect the value of $var outside the function.

In contrast, when you pass an argument by reference, changes to the parameter within the function do affect the value of the argument outside the scope of the function. That's because when you pass an argument by reference, you must pass a variable to the function. Now the parameter in the function refers directly to the value of the variable, meaning that any changes within the function are also visible outside the function. For example:

```
function triple(&$x) {
  $x=$x*3;
  return $x;
}
$var=10;
triple($var);
```

The & that precedes $x in the triple() function definition causes the argument to be passed by reference, so the end result is that $var ends up with a value of 30.

Variable Scope

The scope of a variable is the context within which a variable is available. There are two scopes for variables in PHP. Global variables are available directly from the mainline PHP execution. That is, if you are not inside a function, you can access global variables directly. Unlike most other languages, functions in PHP have their own, completely separate variable scope. Take this example:

```php
<?php
  function test() {
    echo $a;
  }

  $a = "Hello World";
  test();
?>
```

If you run this script you will find that there is no output. This is because the $a you are trying to access inside the test() function is a completely different variable from the global $a you created in the global scope just before calling the function. In order to access a globally-scoped variable from inside a function, you need to tell the function to use the global scope for that particular variable. It can be done with the global keyword like this:

```php
<?php
  function test() {
    global $a;
    echo $a;
  }

  $a = "Hello World";
  test();
?>
```

Alternatively, you can use the $GLOBALS array like this:

```php
<?php
  function test() {
    echo $GLOBALS['a'];
  }
```

```
    $a = "Hello World";
    test();
?>
```

In this last example, the $GLOBALS array is known as a *super-global*, which is a variable that is automatically available in all scopes without needing to be declared global in order to be accessed from within a function.

Static Variables

PHP supports declaring local function variables as static. A static variable retains its value between function calls, but is still accessible only from within the function it is declared in. Static variables can be initialized; this initialization only takes place the first time the static declaration is executed. Static variables are often used as counters, as in this example:

```
function hitcount( )
  static $count = 0;

  if ($count == 0) {
    echo "This is the first access to this page";
  } else {
    echo "This page has been accessed $count times";
  }
  $count++;
}
```

Web-Related Variables

PHP automatically creates variables for all the data it receives in an HTTP request. This can include GET data, POST data, cookie data, and environment variables. The variables are either in PHP's global symbol table or in one of a number of superglobal arrays, depending on the value of the register_globals setting in your *php.ini* file.

In PHP 4.2.0 and after, the default setting for register_globals is off. With register_globals off, all the various variables that are usually available directly in the global symbol table are now available via individual superglobal arrays. There is a limited set of superglobals and they cannot be created from a user-level script. The superglobal array to use depends on the source of the variable. Here is the list:

$_GET

> GET-method variables. These are the variables supplied directly in the URL. For example, with *http://www.example.com/script.php?a=1&b=2*, $_GET['a'] and $_GET['b'] are set to 1 and 2, respectively.

$_POST

> POST-method variables. Form field data from regular POST-method forms.

$_COOKIE

> Any cookies the browser sends end up in this array. The name of the cookie is the key and the cookie value becomes the array value.

$_REQUEST

> This array contains all of these variables (i.e., GET, POST, and cookie). If a variable appears in multiple sources, the order in which they are imported into $_REQUEST is given by the setting of the variables_order *php.ini* directive. The default is 'GPC', which means GET-method variables are imported first, then POST-method variables (overriding any GET-method variables of the same name), and finally cookie variables (overriding the other two).

$_SERVER

> These are variables set by your web server. Traditionally things like DOCUMENT_ROOT, REMOTE_ADDR, REMOTE_PORT, SERVER_NAME, SERVER_PORT, and many others. To get a full list, have a look at your phpinfo() output, or run a script like the following to have a look:

```php
<?php
  foreach($_SERVER as $key=>$val) {
    echo '$_SERVER['.$key."] = $val<br>\n";
  }
?>
```

$_ENV

Any environment variables that were set when you started your web server are available in this array.

$_FILES

For RFC 1867–style file uploads the information for each uploaded file is available in this array. For example, for a file upload form containing:

```
<input name="userfile" type="file">
```

The $_FILES array will look something like this:

```
$_FILES['userfile']['name'] => photo.png
$_FILES['userfile']['type'] => image/png
$_FILES['userfile']['tmp_name'] => /tmp/phpo3kdGt
$_FILES['userfile']['error'] => 0
$_FILES['userfile']['size'] => 158918
```

Note that the 'error' field is new for PHP 4.2.0 and the values are: 0 (no error, file was uploaded); 1 (the uploaded file exceeds the upload_max_filesize directive in *php.ini*); 2 (the uploaded file exceeds the MAX_FILE_SIZE directive that was specified in the HTML form); 3 (the actual number of bytes uploaded was less than the specified upload file size); and 4 (no file was uploaded).

Sessions

Sessions are used to help maintain the values of variables across multiple web pages. This is done by creating a unique session ID that is sent to the client browser. The browser then sends the unique ID back on each page request and PHP uses the ID to fetch the values of all the variables associated with this session.

The session ID is sent back and forth in a cookie or in the URL. By default, PHP tries to use cookies, but if the browser has disabled cookies, PHP falls back to putting the ID in the URL. The *php.ini* directives that affect this are:

session.use_cookies
> When on, PHP will try to use cookies

session.use_trans_sid
> When on, PHP will add the ID to URLs if cookies are not used

The trans_sid code in PHP is rather interesting. It actually parses the entire HTML file and modifies/mangles every link and form to add the session ID. The url_rewriter.tags *php.ini* directive can change how the various elements are mangled.

Writing an application that uses sessions is not hard. You start a session using session_start(), then register the variables you wish to associate with that session. For example:

```php
<?php
  session_start();
  session_register('foo');
  session_register('bar');

  $foo = "Hello";
  $bar = "World";
?>
```

If you put the previous example in a file named *page1.php* and load it in your browser, it sends you a cookie and stores the values of $foo and $bar on the server. If you then load this *page2.php* page:

```php
<?php
  session_start();
  echo "foo = $_SESSION[foo]<br />";
  echo "bar = $_SESSION[bar]<br />";
?>
```

You should see the values of $foo and $bar set in *page1.php*. Note the use of the $_SESSION superglobal. If you have register_globals on, you would be able to access these as $foo and $bar directly.

You can add complex variables such as arrays and objects to sessions as well. The one caveat with putting an object in a session is that you must load the class definition for that object before you call session_start().

A common error people make when using sessions is that they tend to use it as a replacement for authentication—or sometimes as an add-on to authentication. Authenticating a user once as he first enters your site and then using a session ID to identify that user throughout the rest of the site without further authentication can lead to a lot of problems if another person is somehow able to get the session ID. There are a number of ways to get the session ID:

- If you are not using SSL, session IDs may be sniffed
- If you don't have proper entropy in your session IDs, they may be guessed
- If you are using URL-based session IDs, they may end up in proxy logs
- If you are using URL-based session IDs, they may end up bookmarked on publicly-accessible computers

Forcing HTTP Authentication on each page over SSL is the most secure way to avoid this problem, but it tends to be a bit inconvenient. Just keep the above points in mind when building a web application that uses sessions to store users' personal details.

Examples

The best way to understand the power of PHP is to examine some real examples of PHP in action, so we'll look at some common uses of PHP in this section.

Showing the Browser and IP Address

Here is a simple page that prints out the browser string and the IP address of the HTTP request. Create a file with the following content in your web directory, name it something like *example.php3*, and load it in your browser:

```
<html><head><title>PHP Example</title></head>
<body>
    You are using
     <?php echo $_SERVER['HTTP_USER_AGENT'] ?>
    <br />
    and coming from
     <?php echo $_SERVER['REMOTE_ADDR'] ?>
</body></html>
```

You should see something like the following in your browser window:

```
You are using Mozilla/5.0 (X11; U; Linux i686; en-US;
rv:1.1b) Gecko/20020722
and coming from 127.0.0.1
```

Intelligent Form Handling

Here is a slightly more complex example. We are going to create an HTML form that asks the user to enter a name and select one or more interests from a selection box. We could do this in two files, where we separate the actual form from the data handling code, but instead, this example shows how it can be done in a single file:

```
<html><head><title>Form Example</title></head>
<body>
<h1>Form Example</h1>
<?
function show_form($first="", $last="",
                    $interest="") {
 $options = array("Sports", "Business", "Travel",
                  "Shopping", "Computers");
 if(!is_array($interest)) $interest = array();
 ?>
 <form action="form.php" method="POST">
```

```
First Name:
<input type="text" name="first"
       value="<?echo $first?>">
<br />
Last Name:
<input type="text" name="last"
       value="<?echo $last?>">
<br />
Interests:
<select multiple name="interest[]">
<?php
 foreach($options as $option) {
  echo "<option";
  if(in_array($option, $interest)) {
   echo " selected ";
  }
  echo "> $option</option>\n";
 }
?>
</select><br />
<input type=submit>
</form>
<?php } // end of show_form() function

if($_SERVER['REQUEST_METHOD']!='POST') {
 show_form();
} else {
 if(empty($_POST['first']) ||
    empty($_POST['last'])  ||
    empty($_POST['interest'])) {
  echo "<p>You did not fill in all the fields,";
  echo "please try again</p>\n";
  show_form($_POST['first'],$_POST['last'],
            $_POST['interest']);
 }
 else {
  echo "<p>Thank you, $_POST[first] $_POST[last], you ";
  echo 'selected '.
       join(' and ', $_POST['interest']);
  echo " as your interests.</p>\n";
 }
}
?>
</body></html>
```

There are a few things to study carefully in this example. First, we have isolated the display of the actual form to a PHP function called show_form(). This function is intelligent, in that it can take the default value for each of the form elements as an optional argument. If the user does not fill in all the form elements, we use this feature to redisplay the form with whatever values the user has already entered. This means the user only has to fill the fields he missed, which is much better than asking the user to hit the Back button or forcing him to reenter all the fields.

Notice how the file switches back and forth between PHP code and HTML. Right in the middle of defining our show_form() function, we switch back to HTML to avoid having numerous echo statements that just echo normal HTML. Then, when we need a PHP variable, we switch back to PHP code temporarily, just to print the variable.

We've given the multiple-choice <select> element the name interest[]. The [] on the name tells PHP that the data coming from this form element should be treated as an auto-indexed array. This means that PHP automatically gives each element the next sequential index, starting with 0 (assuming the array is empty to begin with).

The final thing to note is the way we determine what to display. We check if the SERVER variable REQUEST_METHOD is set to POST. If it isn't, we know that the user has not submitted the form yet, so we call show_form() without any arguments. This displays the empty form. If $first is set, however, we check to make sure that the $first and $last text fields are not empty and that the user has selected at least one interest.

Web Database Integration

To illustrate a complete database-driven application, we are going to build a little web application that lets people make suggestions and vote on what you should name your new baby. The example uses MySQL, a fast and easy to configure database (see *http://www.mysql.com*), but it can be changed to run on any of the databases that PHP supports.

The schema for our baby-name database looks like this:

```
CREATE TABLE baby_names (
  name varchar(30) NOT NULL,
  votes int(4),
  PRIMARY KEY (name)
);
```

This is in MySQL's query format and can be used directly to create the actual table. It simply defines a text field and an integer field. The text field is for the suggested baby name and the integer field is for the vote count associated with that name. We are making the name field a primary key, which means uniqueness is enforced, so that the same name cannot appear twice in the database.

We want this application to do a number of things. First, it should have a minimal check that prevents someone from voting many times in a row. We do this using a session cookie. Second, we want to show a fancy little barchart that depicts the relative share of the votes that each name has received. The barchart is created using a one pixel by one pixel blue dot GIF image and scaling the image using the height and width settings of the HTML <img> tag. We could also use PHP's built-in image functions to create a fancier-looking bar.

Everything else is relatively straightforward form and database work. We use a couple of shortcuts as well. For example, instead of reading all the entries from the database and adding up the votes in order to get a sum (which we need to calculate the percentages), we ask MySQL to do it for us with its built-in sum( ) function. The part of the code that displays all the names and their votes along with the percentage bar gets a little ugly, but you should be able to follow it. We are simply sending the correct HTML table tags before and after the various data we have fetched from the database.

Here's the full example:

```php
<?
  if($vote && !$already_voted)
    SetCookie('already_voted',1);
?>
<html><head><title>Name the Baby</title>
</head><h3>Name the Baby</h3>
<form action="baby.php" method="POST">
<p>Suggestion:
<input type="text" name="new_name"></p>
<input type="submit"
       value="Submit idea and/or vote">
<?
 mysql_pconnect("localhost","","");
 $db = "test";
 $table = "baby_names";

 if($new_name) {
  if(!mysql_db_query($db, "insert into $table
      values ('$new_name',0)")) {
    echo mysql_errno().': '.
         mysql_error()."<br />\n";
  }
 }
 if($vote && $already_voted) {
  echo '<p><b>Hey, you voted already ';
  echo "Vote ignored.</b></p>\n";
 }
 else if($vote) {
  if(!mysql_db_query($db,
       "update $table set votes=votes+1
        where name='$vote'")) {
   echo mysql_errno().': '.
        mysql_error()."<br />\n";
  }
 }
 $result=mysql_db_query($db,
     "select sum(votes) as sum from $table");
 if($result) {
  $sum = (int) mysql_result($result,0,"sum");
  mysql_free_result($result);
 }

 $result=mysql_db_query($db,
   "select * from $table order by votes DESC");
```

```php
  echo <<<EOD
   <table border="0"><tr><th>Vote</th>
   <th>Idea</th><th colspan="2">Votes</th>
   </tr>
EOD;
  while($row=mysql_fetch_row($result)) {
   echo <<<FOO
    <tr><td align="center">
    <input type="radio"
           name="vote" value="$row[0]"></td>
    <td>$row[0]</td>
    <td align="right">$row[1]</td>
    <td>
FOO;
   if($sum && (int)$row[1]) {
   $per = (int)(100 * $row[1]/$sum);
   echo '<img src="bline.gif" height=12 ';
   echo "width=$per> $per %</td>";
   }
   echo "</tr>\n";
   }
  echo "</table>\n";
  mysql_free_result($result);
?>
<input type="submit"
       value="Submit idea and/or vote" />
<input type="reset" />
</form>
</body></html>
```

Function Reference

The rest of this book provides an alphabetical summary of the functions that are available in PHP. The synopsis for each function lists the expected argument types for the function, its return type, and the version of PHP in which the function was introduced. The possible types are int, double, string, array, void, and mixed. mixed means that the argument or return type can be of any type. Optional arguments are shown in square brackets. Note that PHP didn't start tracking version numbers for functions until PHP 3.0, so functions that are listed as 3.0 are likely to have existed in Version 2.x.

As of PHP 4.3, approximately 2,750 functions came bundled with PHP. The bulk of these are in optional extensions. Out of these functions, I selected 1,404 for this pocket reference. Even with close to half the functions cut, I'm still pushing the limits of what the average pocket can hold without busting a few seams. Here's a list of the function groups that survived the cut, followed by the ones that didn't:

In

Apache, array, assert, aspell/pspell, base64, bcmath, bz2, calendar, crack, crc32, crypt, ctype, curl, date/time, dba, db, dbx, directory, DNS, exec, exif, file, ftp, gd, gettext, gmp, HTML, iconv, imap, iptc, java, lcg, ldap, link, mail, math, md5, mbstring, mcrypt, mhash, MySQL, Oracle 8, PDF, Perl regex, PostgreSQL, Posix, process control, recode, session, shmop, snmp, sockets, various standard built-in, syslog, SYSV shared mem/sem/msg, xml, xslt, zip, zlib.

Out

COM, cpdf, Cybercash, Cybermut, Cyrus, dbase, direct io, DomXML, Frontbase, FDF, Filepro, Fribidi, Hyperwave, ICAP, Informix, Ingres, Interbase, ircg, mbregex, MCAL, MCVE, Ming, mnogosearch, msession, mSQL, mssql, ncurses, Lotus Notes, Birdstep, ODBC, OpenSSL, Oracle 7, Ovrimos, Payflow Pro, QTDom, readline, aggregation, browscap, cyrillic conversions, libswf, Sybase, Tokenizer, VPopMail, Win32 API, WDDX, XMLRPC, Yaz, YellowPages.

If your favorite functions were left out, please don't take it personally. I had a lot of tough choices to make. One of the hardest was DomXML. At 114 functions, the DomXML extension is huge and there just wasn't room. Leaving out the cool Ming functions was difficult as well. Please do check out the online manual at *http://www.php.net/manual* for more on both of these extensions and also all the others you see listed here.

int abs(int number)   *3.0*
> Returns the absolute value of the number

float acos(float number)   *3.0*
> Returns the arc cosine of the number in radians

float acosh(float number)   *4.1.0*
> Returns the inverse hyperbolic cosine of the number (i.e., the value whose hyperbolic cosine is number)

string addcslashes(string str, string charlist)   *4.0*
> Escapes all characters mentioned in charlist with back-slashes, creating octal representations if asked to backslash characters with their 8th bit set or with an ASCII value greater than 32 (except '\n', '\r', '\t', etc.)

string addslashes(string str)   *3.0*
> Escapes single quotes, double quotes, and backslash characters in a string with backslashes

AND   *4.0*
> Language keyword that is similar to the && operator, except with lower precedence

bool apache_child_terminate(void)   *4.0.5*
> Terminates Apache process after this request

object apache_lookup_uri(string URI)   *3.0.4*
> Performs a partial request of the given URI to obtain information about it

string apache_note(string note_name[, string note_value])   *3.0.2*
> Gets and sets Apache request notes

array apache_request_headers(void)   *4.3.0*
> Fetches all HTTP request headers

array apache_response_headers(void)   *4.3.0*
> Fetches all HTTP response headers

bool apache_setenv(string variable, string value[, bool walk_to_top])   *4.1.0*
> Sets an Apache subprocess_env variable

array array([mixed var[, ...]])   *3.0*
> Creates an array

array array_change_key_case(array input[, int case=CASE_LOWER])   *4.1.0*
> Returns an array with all string keys lowercased (or uppercased)

array array_chunk(array input, int size[, bool preserve_keys])   *4.1.0*
> Splits array into chunks

array array_count_values(array input)   *4.0*
> Returns the value as key and the frequency of that value in input as value

array array_diff(array arr1, array arr2[, array ...])   *4.0.1*
> Returns the entries of arr1 that have values that are not present in any of the others arguments

array array_fill(int start_key, int num, mixed val)   *4.1.0*
> Creates an array containing num elements starting with index start_key each initialized to val

array array_filter(array input[, mixed callback])   *4.0.6*
> Filters elements from the array via the callback

array array_flip(array input)   *4.0*
> Returns array with key/value pairs flipped

array array_intersect(array arr1, array arr2[, array ...])   *4.0.1*
> Returns the entries of arr1 that have values that are present in all the other arguments

bool array_key_exists(mixed key, array search)   *4.1.0*
> Checks if the given key or index exists in the array

array array_keys(array input[, mixed search_value])   *4.0*
> Returns just the keys from the input array, optionally for only the specified search_value

array array_map(mixed callback, array input1[, array input2 ,...])   *4.0.6*
> Applies the callback to the elements in the given arrays

array array_merge(array arr1, array arr2[, array ...])   *4.0*
> Merges elements from passed arrays into one array

array array_merge_recursive(array arr1, array arr2[, array ...])   *4.0.1*
> Recursively merges elements from passed arrays into one array

bool array_multisort(array ar1[, SORT_ASC|SORT_DESC[, SORT_REGULAR|
SORT_NUMERIC|SORT_STRING]][, array ar2[, SORT_ASC|SORT_DESC[,
SORT_REGULAR|SORT_NUMERIC|SORT_STRING]], ...])   4.0

> Sorts multiple arrays at once similar to how ORDER BY clause
> works in SQL

array array_pad(array input, int pad_size, mixed pad_value)   4.0

> Returns a copy of input array padded with pad_value to size
> pad_size

mixed array_pop(array stack)   4.0

> Pops an element off the end of the array

int array_push(array stack, mixed var[, mixed ...])   4.0

> Pushes elements onto the end of the array

mixed array_rand(array input[, int num_req])   4.0

> Returns key/keys for random entry/entries in the array

mixed array_reduce(array input, mixed callback[, int initial])   4.0.5

> Iteratively reduces the array to a single value via the callback

array array_reverse(array input[, bool preserve keys])   4.0

> Returns input as a new array with the order of the entries
> reversed

mixed array_search(mixed needle, array haystack[, bool strict])   4.0.5

> Searches the array for a given value and returns the corre-
> sponding key if successful

mixed array_shift(array stack)   4.0

> Pops an element off the beginning of the array

array array_slice(array input, int offset[, int length])   4.0

> Returns elements specified by offset and length

array array_splice(array input, int offset[, int length[, array replacement]])   4.0

> Removes the elements designated by offset and length and
> replaces them with supplied array

mixed array_sum(array input)   4.0.4

> Returns the sum of the array entries

array array_unique(array input)   4.0.1

> Removes duplicate values from array

---

int array_unshift(array stack, mixed var[, mixed ...])   *4.0*
    Pushes elements onto the beginning of the array

array array_values(array input)   *4.0*
    Returns just the values from the input array

bool array_walk(array input, string funcname[, mixed userdata])   *3.0.3*
    Applies a user function to every member of an array

bool arsort(array array_arg[, int sort_flags])   *3.0*
    Sorts an array in reverse order and maintains index association

float asin(float number)   *3.0*
    Returns the arc sine of the number in radians

float asinh(float number)   *4.1.0*
    Returns the inverse hyperbolic sine of the number (i.e., the value whose hyperbolic sine is number)

bool asort(array array_arg[, int sort_flags])   *3.0*
    Sorts an array and maintains index association

int aspell_check(aspell int, string word)   *3.0.7*
    Returns if word is valid

int aspell_check_raw(aspell int, string word)   *3.0.7*
    Returns if word is valid, ignoring case and without trying to trim it in any way

int aspell_new(string master[, string personal])   *3.0.7*
    Loads a dictionary

array aspell_suggest(aspell int, string word)   *3.0.7*
    Returns an array of spelling suggestions

int assert(string|bool assertion)   *4.0*
    Checks if assertion is false

mixed assert_options(int what[, mixed value])   *4.0*
    Sets or gets the various assert flags

float atan(float number)   *3.0*
    Returns the arc tangent of the number in radians

float atan2(float y, float x)   *3.0.5*
    Returns the arc tangent of y/x, with the resulting quadrant determined by the signs of y and x

float atanh(float number)   *4.1.0*
> Returns the inverse hyperbolic tangent of the number (i.e., the value whose hyperbolic tangent is number)

string base64_decode(string str)   *3.0*
> Decodes string using MIME base64 algorithm

string base64_encode(string str)   *3.0*
> Encodes string using MIME base64 algorithm

string base_convert(string number, int frombase, int tobase)   *3.0.6*
> Converts a number in a string from any base to any other base (where both bases are less than or equal to 36)

string basename(string path[, string suffix])   *3.0*
> Returns the filename component of the path

string bcadd(string left_operand, string right_operand[, int scale])   *3.0*
> Returns the sum of two arbitrary precision numbers

string bccomp(string left_operand, string right_operand[, int scale])   *3.0*
> Compares two arbitrary precision numbers

string bcdiv(string left_operand, string right_operand[, int scale])   *3.0*
> Returns the quotient of two arbitrary precision numbers (division)

string bcmod(string left_operand, string right_operand)   *3.0*
> Returns the modulus of the two arbitrary precision operands

string bcmul(string left_operand, string right_operand[, int scale])   *3.0*
> Returns the product of two arbitrary precision numbers

string bcpow(string x, string y[, int scale])   *3.0*
> Returns the value of an arbitrary precision number raised to the power of another arbitrary precision number

string bcscale(int scale)   *3.0*
> Sets default scale parameter for all BC math functions

string bcsqrt(string operand[, int scale])   *3.0*
> Returns the square root of an arbitrary precision number

string bcsub(string left_operand, string right_operand[, int scale])   *3.0*
> Returns the difference between two arbitrary precision numbers

string bin2hex(string data)   *3.0.9*
> Converts the binary representation of data to hexadecimal

---

string bind_textdomain_codeset (string domain, string codeset)   *4.1.0*
  Specifies the character encoding in which the messages from
  the DOMAIN message catalog will be returned

int bindec(string binary_number)   *3.0*
  Returns the decimal equivalent of a binary number

string bindtextdomain(string domain_name, string dir)   *3.0.7*
  Binds to the text domain domain_name, looking for transla-
  tions in dir; returns the current domain

break   *3.0*
  Language keyword used inside switch statements and loops

string bzcompress(string source[, int blocksize100k[, int workfactor]])   *4.0.4*
  Compresses a string into BZip2 encoded data

string bzdecompress(string source[, int small])   *4.0.4*
  Decompresses BZip2 compressed data

int bzerrno(resource bz)   *4.0.4*
  Returns the error number

array bzerror(resource bz)   *4.0.4*
  Returns the error number and error string in an associative
  array

string bzerrstr(resource bz)   *4.0.4*
  Returns the error string

resource bzopen(string|int file|fp, string mode)   *4.0.4*
  Opens a new BZip2 stream

string bzread(int bz[, int length])   *4.0.4*
  Reads up to length bytes from a BZip2 stream, or 1,024 bytes
  if length is not specified

int cal_days_in_month(int calendar, int month, int year)   *4.1.0*
  Returns the number of days in a month for a given year and
  calendar

array cal_from_jd(int jd, int calendar)   *4.1.0*
  Converts from Julian day count to a supported calendar and
  returns extended information

array cal_info(int calendar)   *4.1.0*
  Returns information about a particular calendar

int cal_to_jd(int calendar, int month, int day, int year)   *4.1.0*
    Converts from a supported calendar to Julian day count

mixed call_user_func(string function_name[, mixed parmeter][, mixed ...]) *3.0.3*
    Calls a user function that is the first parameter

mixed call_user_func_array(string function_name, array parameters)   *4.0.4*
    Calls a user function that is the first parameter with the arguments contained in array

mixed call_user_method(string method_name, mixed object[, mixed parameter][, mixed ...])   *3.0.3*
    Calls a user method on a specific object or class

mixed call_user_method_array(string method_name, mixed object, array params)   *4.0.5*
    Calls a user method on a specific object or class using a parameter array

case arg: *3.0*
    Language keyword used inside a switch statement

float ceil(float number)   *3.0*
    Returns the next highest integer value of the number

bool chdir(string directory)   *3.0*
    Changes the current directory

bool checkdate(int month, int day, int year)   *3.0*
    Returns true if passed a valid date in the Gregorian calendar

int checkdnsrr(string host[, string type])   *3.0*
    Checks DNS records corresponding to a given Internet host name or IP address

bool chgrp(string filename, mixed group)   *3.0*
    Changes file group

bool chmod(string filename, int mode)   *3.0*
    Changes file mode

bool chown (string filename, mixed user)   *3.0*
    Changes file owner

string chr(int ascii)   *3.0*
    Converts ASCII code to a character

bool chroot(string directory)   *4.0.5*
Changes root directory

string chunk_split(string str[, int chunklen[, string ending]])   *3.0.6*
Returns split line

class class_name   *3.0*
Language keyword that defines a class

bool class_exists(string classname)   *4.0*
Checks if the class exists

void clearstatcache(void)   *3.0*
Clears file stat cache

void closedir([resource dir_handle])   *3.0*
Closes directory connection identified by dir handle

bool closelog(void)   *3.0*
Closes connection to system logger

array compact(mixed var_names[, mixed ...])   *4.0*
Creates a hash containing variables and their values

int connection_aborted(void)   *3.0.7*
Returns true if client disconnected

int connection_status(void)   *3.0.7*
Returns the connection status bitfield

mixed constant(string const_name)   *4.0.4*
Returns the associated value, given the name of a constant

continue   *3.0*
Language keyword used inside loops to skip to the next iteration

bool copy(string source_file, string destination_file)   *3.0*
Copies a file

float cos(float number)   *3.0*
Returns the cosine of the number in radians

float cosh(float number)   *4.1.0*
Returns the hyperbolic cosine of the number

int count(mixed var[, int mode])   *3.0*
Counts the number of elements in a variable (usually an array)

mixed count_chars(string input[, int mode])   *4.0*
    Returns information about what characters are used in input

string crack_check([int dictionary,] string password)   *4.0.5*
    Performs an obscure check with the given password

string crack_closedict([int link_identifier])   *4.0.5*
    Closes an open *cracklib* dictionary

string crack_getlastmessage(void)   *4.0.5*
    Returns the message from the last obscure check

string crack_opendict(string dictionary)   *4.0.5*
    Opens a new *cracklib* dictionary

string crc32(string str)   *4.0.1*
    Calculates the crc32 polynomial of a string

string create_function(string args, string code)   *4.0.1*
    Creates an anonymous function and returns its name

string crypt(string str[, string salt])   *3.0*
    Encrypts a string

bool ctype_alnum(mixed c)   *4.0.4*
    Checks for alphanumeric character(s)

bool ctype_alpha(mixed c)   *4.0.4*
    Checks for alphabetic character(s)

bool ctype_cntrl(mixed c)   *4.0.4*
    Checks for control character(s)

bool ctype_digit(mixed c)   *4.0.4*
    Checks for numeric character(s)

bool ctype_graph(mixed c)   *4.0.4*
    Checks for any printable character(s) except space

bool ctype_lower(mixed c)   *4.0.4*
    Checks for lowercase character(s)

bool ctype_print(mixed c)   *4.0.4*
    Checks for printable character(s)

bool ctype_punct(mixed c)   *4.0.4*
    Checks for any printable character that is not whitespace or
    an alphanumeric character

---

bool ctype_space(mixed c) *4.0.4*
    Checks for whitespace character(s)

bool ctype_upper(mixed c) *4.0.4*
    Checks for uppercase character(s)

bool ctype_xdigit(mixed c) *4.0.4*
    Checks for character(s) representing a hexadecimal digit

void curl_close(resource ch) *4.0.2*
    Closes a CURL session

int curl_errno(resource ch) *4.0.3*
    Returns an integer containing the last error number

string curl_error(resource ch) *4.0.3*
    Returns a string contain the last error for the current session

bool curl_exec(resource ch) *4.0.2*
    Performs a CURL session

string curl_getinfo(resource ch, int opt) *4.0.4*
    Gets information regarding a specific transfer

resource curl_init([string url]) *4.0.2*
    Initializes a CURL session

bool curl_setopt(resource ch, string option, mixed value) *4.0.2*
    Sets an option for a CURL transfer

string curl_version(void) *4.0.2*
    Returns the CURL version string.

mixed current(array array_arg) *3.0*
    Returns the element currently pointed to by the internal array pointer

string date(string format[, int timestamp]) *3.0*
    Formats a local time/date

void dba_close(int handle) *3.0.8*
    Closes the database

bool dba_delete(string key, int handle) *3.0.8*
    Deletes the entry associated with key

bool dba_exists(string key, int handle) *3.0.8*
    Checks if the specified key exists

string dba_fetch(string key, int handle) *3.0.8*
    Fetches the data associated with key

string dba_firstkey(int handle) *3.0.8*
    Resets the internal key pointer and returns the first key

bool dba_insert(string key, string value, int handle) *3.0.8*
    Inserts value as key; returns false if key exists already

string dba_nextkey(int handle) *3.0.8*
    Returns the next key

int dba_open(string path, string mode, string handlername[, string ...]) *3.0.8*
    Opens path using the specified handler in specified mode

bool dba_optimize(int handle) *3.0.8*
    Optimizes database

int dba_popen(string path, string mode, string handlername[, string ...]) *3.0.8*
    Opens path persistently using the specified handler in specified mode

bool dba_replace(string key, string value, int handle) *3.0.8*
    Inserts value as key; replaces key if key exists already

bool dba_sync(int handle) *3.0.8*
    Synchronizes database

string dblist(void) *3.0*
    Describes the DBM-compatible library being used

bool dbmclose(int dbm_identifier) *3.0*
    Closes a DBM database

int dbmdelete(int dbm_identifier, string key) *3.0*
    Deletes the value for a key from a DBM database

int dbmexists(int dbm_identifier, string key) *3.0*
    Tells if a value exists for a key in a DBM database

string dbmfetch(int dbm_identifier, string key) *3.0*
    Fetches a value for a key from a DBM database

string dbmfirstkey(int dbm_identifier) *3.0*
    Retrieves the first key from a DBM database

int dbminsert(int dbm_identifier, string key, string value) *3.0*
    Inserts a value for a key in a DBM database

string dbmnextkey(int dbm_identifier, string key) *3.0*
    Retrieves the next key from a DBM database

int dbmopen(string filename, string mode) *3.0*
    Opens a DBM database

int dbmreplace(int dbm_identifier, string key, string value) *3.0*
    Replaces the value for a key in a DBM database

bool dbx_close(dbx_link_object dbx_link) *4.0.6*
    Closes an open connection/database

int dbx_compare(array row_x, array row_y, string columnname[, int flags]) *4.1.0*
    Compares two rows for sorting purposes

dbx_link_object dbx_connect(string module_name, string host, string db, string username, string password[, bool persistent]) *4.0.6*
    Opens a connection/database; returns dbx_link_object on success or 0 on failure

void dbx_error(dbx_link_object dbx_link) *4.0.6*
    Reports the error message of the latest function call in the module

dbx_result_object dbx_query(dbx_link_object dbx_link, string sql_statement[, long flags]) *4.0.6*
    Sends a query and fetches all results; returns a dbx_link_object on success or 0 on failure

int dbx_sort(object dbx_result, string compare_function_name) *4.0.6*
    Sorts a result from dbx_query() by a custom sort function

string dcgettext(string domain_name, string msgid, long category) *3.0.7*
    Returns the translation of msgid for domain_name and category or msgid unaltered if a translation does not exist

string dcngettext (string domain, string msgid1, string msgid2, int n, int category) *4.1.0*
    Plural version of dcgettext()

void debug_zval_dump(mixed var) *4.1.0*
    Dumps a string representation of an internal Zend value to output

string decbin(int decimal_number) *3.0*
    Returns a string containing a binary representation of the number

string dechex(int decimal_number) *3.0*
Returns a string containing a hexadecimal representation of the number

declare(directive) *4.0.2*
Language keyword used to mark a block of code; only used for ticks at this point

string decoct(int decimal_number) *3.0*
Returns a string containing an octal representation of the number

default: *3.0*
Language keyword used inside a switch statement

bool define(string constant_name, mixed value, case_sensitive=true) *3.0*
Defines a new constant

void define_syslog_variables(void) *3.0*
Initializes all syslog-related variables

bool defined(string constant_name) *3.0*
Checks whether a constant exists

float deg2rad(float number) *3.0.4*
Converts the number in degrees to the radian equivalent

string dgettext(string domain_name, string msgid) *3.0.7*
Returns the translation of msgid for domain_name or msgid unaltered if a translation does not exist

object dir(string directory) *3.0*
Directory class with properties for handle and class and methods to read, rewind, and close

string dirname(string path) *3.0*
Returns the directory name component of the path

float disk_free_space(string path) *4.1.0*
Gets free disk space for filesystem that path is on

float disk_total_space(string path) *4.1.0*
Gets total disk space for filesystem that path is on

int dl(string extension_filename) *3.0*
Loads a PHP extension at runtime

---

string dngettext (string domain, string msgid1, string msgid2, int count)   *4.1.0*
> Plural version of dgettext( )

do   *3.0*
> Language keyword that forms the start of a do/while loop

array each(array arr)   *3.0*
> Returns the current key/value pair in the passed array and advances the pointer to the next element

int easter_date([int year])   *3.0.9*
> Returns the timestamp of midnight on Easter of a given year (defaults to current year)

int easter_days([int year, [int method]])   *3.0.9*
> Returns the number of days after March 21 that Easter falls on for a given year (defaults to current year)

echo string arg1[, string argn...]   *3.0*
> Outputs one or more strings

else   *3.0*
> Language keyword that reverses the current condition

elseif(cond)   *3.0*
> Language keyword that tests a condition only if current condition was not met

bool empty(mixed var)   *3.0*
> Determines whether a variable is empty

mixed end(array array_arg)   *3.0*
> Advances array argument's internal pointer to the last element and returns it

enddeclare   *4.0.2*
> Language keyword that ends a declare: block

endfor   *3.0*
> Language keyword that ends a for: block

endforeach   *4.0*
> Language keyword that ends a foreach: block

endif   *3.0*
> Language keyword that ends an if: block

endswitch *3.0*
> Language keyword that ends a switch: block

endwhile *3.0*
> Language keyword that ends a while: block

int ereg(string pattern, string string[, array registers]) *3.0*
> Performs a regular expression match

string ereg_replace(string pattern, string replacement, string string) *3.0*
> Performs a regular expression replacement

int eregi(string pattern, string string[, array registers]) *3.0*
> Performs a case-insensitive regular expression match

string eregi_replace(string pattern, string replacement, string string) *3.0*
> Performs a case-insensitive regular expression replacement

bool error_log(string message, int message_type[, string destination]
[, string extra_headers]) *3.0*
> Sends an error message somewhere

int error_reporting(int new_error_level=null) *3.0*
> Returns the current error_reporting level, and, if an argument was passed, changes to the new level

string escapeshellarg(string arg) *4.0.3*
> Quotes and escapes an argument for use in a shell command

string escapeshellcmd(string command) *3.0*
> Escapes shell metacharacters

mixed eval(string code_str) *3.0*
> Evaluates a string as PHP code

string exec(string command[, array output[, int return_value]]) *3.0*
> Executes an external program

int exif_imagetype(string imagefile) *4.3.0*
> Gets the type of an image

array|false exif_read_data(string filename[, sections_needed
[, sub_arrays[, read_thumbnail]]]) *4.1.0*
> Reads header data from the JPEG/TIFF image filename and optionally reads the internal thumbnails

string|false exif_tagname(index) *4.1.0*
> Gets header name for index or false if not defined

---

string|false exif_thumbnail(string filename[, &width,
&height[, &imagetype]]) *4.1.0*
>   Reads the embedded thumbnail

exit [([mixed status])] *3.0*
>   Language keyword that terminates execution of the script and
>   prints status just before exiting

float exp(float number) *3.0*
>   Returns *e* raised to the power of the number

array explode(string separator, string str[, int limit]) *3.0*
>   Splits a string on string separator and returns an array of
>   components

float expm1(float number) *4.1.0*
>   Returns exp(number) - 1, computed in a way that is accurate
>   even when the value of number is close to zero

extends *3.0*
>   Language keyword used in a class definition to extend from a
>   parent class

bool extension_loaded(string extension_name) *3.0.10*
>   Returns true if the named extension is loaded

int extract(array var_array[, int extract_type[, string prefix]]) *3.0.7*
>   Imports variables into symbol table from an array

int ezmlm_hash(string addr) *3.0.17*
>   Calculate EZMLM list hash value

bool fclose(resource fp) *3.0*
>   Closes an open file pointer

bool feof(resource fp) *3.0*
>   Tests for end-of-file on a file pointer

bool fflush(resource fp) *4.0.1*
>   Flushes output

string fgetc(resource fp) *3.0*
>   Gets a character from file pointer

array fgetcsv(resource fp, int length[, string delimiter[, string enclosure]]) *3.0.8*
>   Gets a line from file pointer and parses for CSV fields

string fgets(resource fp[, int length])   *3.0*
    Gets a line from file pointer

string fgetss(resource fp, int length[, string allowable_tags])   *3.0*
    Gets a line from file pointer and strips HTML tags

array file(string filename[, bool use_include_path])   *3.0*
    Reads entire file into an array

bool file_exists(string filename)   *3.0*
    Returns true if filename exists

string file_get_contents(string filename[, bool use_include_path])   *4.3.0*
    Reads the entire file into a string

resource file_get_wrapper_data(resource fp)   *4.3.0*
    Retrieves header/metadata from wrapped file pointer

bool file_register_wrapper(string protocol, string classname)   *4.3.0*
    Registers a custom URL protocol handler class

int fileatime(string filename)   *3.0*
    Gets last access time of file

int filectime(string filename)   *3.0*
    Gets inode modification time of file

int filegroup(string filename)   *3.0*
    Gets file group

int fileinode(string filename)   *3.0*
    Gets file inode

int filemtime(string filename)   *3.0*
    Gets last modification time of file

int fileowner(string filename)   *3.0*
    Gets file owner

int fileperms(string filename)   *3.0*
    Gets file permissions

int filesize(string filename)   *3.0*
    Gets file size

string filetype(string filename)   *3.0*
    Gets file type

float floatval(mixed var) 4.1.0
> Gets the float value of a variable

bool flock(resource fp, int operation[, int &wouldblock]) 3.0.7
> Provides portable file locking

float floor(float number) 3.0
> Returns the next lowest integer value from the number

void flush(void) 3.0
> Flushes the output buffer

float fmod(float x, float y) 4.1.0
> Returns the remainder of dividing x by y as a float

bool fnmatch(string pattern, string filename[, int flags]) 4.3.0
> Matches filename against pattern

resource fopen(string filename, string mode[, bool use_include_path [, resource context]]) 3.0
> Opens a file or a URL and returns a file pointer

for(init; cond; inc) 3.0
> Language keyword that implements a traditional for loop

foreach(array as key=>value) 4.0
> Language keyword that iterates through array and assigns each element to key and value

int fpassthru(resource fp) 3.0
> Outputs all remaining data from a file pointer

string fread(resource fp, int length) 3.0
> Provides a binary-safe file read

int frenchtojd(int month, int day, int year) 3.0
> Converts a French Republic calendar date to Julian day count

mixed fscanf(string str, string format[, string ...]) 4.0.1
> Implements a mostly ANSI-compatible fscanf( )

int fseek(resource fp, int offset[, int whence]) 3.0
> Seeks on a file pointer

int fsockopen(string hostname, int port[, int errno[, string errstr [, float timeout]]]) 3.0
> Opens an Internet or Unix domain socket connection

int fstat(resource fp)　　　　　　　　　　　　　　　*4.0*
  Performs stat( ) on a filehandle

int ftell(resource fp)　　　　　　　　　　　　　　　*3.0*
  Gets file pointer's read/write position

int ftok(string pathname, string proj)　　　　　　　*4.1.0*
  Converts a pathname and a project identifier to a System V
  IPC key

int ftp_async_continue(resource stream)　　　　　　*4.3.0*
  Continues retrieving/sending a file asynchronously

bool ftp_async_fget(resource stream, resource fp, string remote_file,
int mode[, int resumepos])　　　　　　　　　　　　*4.3.0*
  Retrieves a file from the FTP server asynchronously and writes
  it to an open file

bool ftp_async_fput(resource stream, string remote_file, resource fp,
int mode[, int startpos])　　　　　　　　　　　　　*4.3.0*
  Stores a file from an open file to the FTP server
  asynchronously

int ftp_async_get(resource stream, string local_file, string remote_file,
int mode[, int resume_pos])　　　　　　　　　　　　*4.3.0*
  Retrieves a file from the FTP server asynchronously and writes
  it to a local file

bool ftp_async_put(resource stream, string remote_file, string local_file,
int mode[, int startpos])　　　　　　　　　　　　　*4.3.0*
  Stores a file on the FTP server

bool ftp_cdup(resource stream)　　　　　　　　　　*3.0.13*
  Changes to the parent directory

bool ftp_chdir(resource stream, string directory)　　*3.0.13*
  Changes directories

void ftp_close(resource stream)　　　　　　　　　　*4.1.0*
  Closes the FTP stream

resource ftp_connect(string host[, int port[, int timeout)]])　*3.0.13*
  Opens an FTP stream

bool ftp_delete(resource stream, string file)　　　　*3.0.13*
  Deletes a file

---

bool ftp_exec(resource stream, string command)   *4.0.3*
    Requests execution of a program on the FTP server

bool ftp_fget(resource stream, resource fp, string remote_file, int mode
[, int resumepos])   *3.0.13*
    Retrieves a file from the FTP server and writes it to an open file

bool ftp_fput(resource stream, string remote_file, resource fp,
int mode[, int startpos])   *3.0.13*
    Stores a file from an open file to the FTP server

bool ftp_get(resource stream, string local_file, string remote_file,
int mode[, int resume_pos])   *3.0.13*
    Retrieves a file from the FTP server and writes it to a local file

mixed ftp_get_option(resource stream, int option)   *4.1.0*
    Gets an FTP option

bool ftp_login(resource stream, string username, string password)   *3.0.13*
    Logs into the FTP server

int ftp_mdtm(resource stream, string filename)   *3.0.13*
    Returns the last modification time of the file or −1 on error

string ftp_mkdir(resource stream, string directory)   *3.0.13*
    Creates a directory and returns the absolute path for the new directory or false on error

array ftp_nlist(resource stream, string directory)   *3.0.13*
    Returns an array of filenames in the given directory

bool ftp_pasv(resource stream, bool pasv)   *3.0.13*
    Turns passive mode on or off

bool ftp_put(resource stream, string remote_file, string local_file,
int mode[, int startpos])   *3.0.13*
    Stores a file on the FTP server

string ftp_pwd(resource stream)   *3.0.13*
    Returns the present working directory

array ftp_rawlist(resource stream, string directory[, bool recursive])   *3.0.13*
    Returns a detailed listing of a directory as an array of output lines

bool ftp_rename(resource stream, string src, string dest)   *3.0.13*
    Renames the given file to a new path

bool ftp_rmdir(resource stream, string directory)   *3.0.13*
    Removes a directory

bool ftp_set_option(resource stream, int option, mixed value)   *4.1.0*
    Sets an FTP option

bool ftp_site(resource stream, string cmd)   *3.0.15*
    Sends a site command to the server

int ftp_size(resource stream, string filename)   *3.0.13*
    Returns the size of the file or −1 on error

string ftp_systype(resource stream)   *3.0.13*
    Returns the system type identifier

int ftruncate(resource fp, int size)   *4.0*
    Truncates file to size length

mixed func_get_arg(int arg_num)   *4.0*
    Gets the specified argument that was passed to the function

array func_get_args()   *4.0*
    Gets an array of the arguments that were passed to the function

int func_num_args(void)   *4.0*
    Gets the number of arguments that were passed to the function

function func_name($arg1, $arg2, ...)   *3.0*
    Language keyword used to define a function

bool function_exists(string function_name)   *3.0.7*
    Checks if the function exists

int fwrite(resource fp, string str[, int length])   *3.0*
    Provides a binary-safe file write

string get_cfg_var(string option_name)   *3.0*
    Gets the value of a PHP configuration option

string get_class(object object)   *4.0*
    Retrieves the class name

array get_class_methods(mixed class)   *4.0*
    Returns an array of method names for class or class instance

array get_class_vars(string class_name)   *4.0*
    Returns an array of default properties of the class

---

string get_current_user(void)   *3.0*
    Gets the name of the owner of the current PHP script

array get_declared_classes(void)   *4.0*
    Returns an array of all declared classes

array get_defined_constants(void)   *4.1.0*
    Returns an array containing the names and values of all
    defined constants

array get_defined_functions(void)   *4.0.4*
    Returns an array of all defined functions

array get_defined_vars(void)   *4.0.4*
    Returns an associative array of names and values of all
    currently defined variable names (variables in the current
    scope)

array get_extension_funcs(string extension_name)   *4.0*
    Returns an array with the names of functions belonging to the
    named extension

array get_html_translation_table([int table[, int quote_style]])   *4.0*
    Returns the internal translation table used by
    htmlspecialchars() and htmlentities()

array get_included_files(void)   *4.0*
    Returns an array with the filenames that were included with
    include_once

array get_loaded_extensions(void)   *4.0*
    Returns an array containing names of loaded extensions

int get_magic_quotes_gpc(void)   *3.0.6*
    Gets the active configuration setting of magic_quotes_gpc

int get_magic_quotes_runtime(void)   *3.0.6*
    Gets the active configuration setting of magic_quotes_runtime

array get_meta_tags(string filename[, bool use_include_path])   *3.0.4*
    Extracts all meta tag content attributes from a file and returns
    an array

array get_object_vars(object obj)   *4.0*
    Returns an array of object properties

string get_parent_class(mixed object)   *4.0*
    Retrieves the parent class name for object or class

---

string get_resource_type(resource res)   *4.0.2*
    Gets the resource type name for a given resource

array getallheaders(void)   *3.0*
    An alias for `apache_request_headers()`

mixed getcwd(void)   *4.0*
    Gets the current directory

array getdate([int timestamp])   *3.0*
    Gets date/time information

string getenv(string varname)   *3.0*
    Gets the value of an environment variable

string gethostbyaddr(string ip_address)   *3.0*
    Gets the Internet hostname corresponding to a given IP address

string gethostbyname(string hostname)   *3.0*
    Gets the IP address corresponding to a given Internet hostname

array gethostbynamel(string hostname)   *3.0*
    Returns a list of IP addresses that a given hostname resolves to

array getimagesize(string imagefile[, array info])   *3.0*
    Gets the size of an image as a four-element array

int getlastmod(void)   *3.0*
    Gets time of last page modification

int getmxrr(string hostname, array mxhosts[, array weight])   *3.0*
    Gets MX records corresponding to a given Internet hostname

int getmygid(void)   *4.1.0*
    Gets PHP script owner's group ID

int getmyinode(void)   *3.0*
    Gets the inode of the current script being parsed

int getmypid(void)   *3.0*
    Gets current process ID

int getmyuid(void)   *3.0*
    Gets PHP script owner's user ID

---

int getprotobyname(string name)   *4.0*

Returns protocol number associated with name as per */etc/protocols*

string getprotobynumber(int proto)   *4.0*

Returns protocol name associated with protocol number proto

int getrandmax(void)   *3.0*

Returns the maximum value a random number can have

array getrusage([int who])   *3.0.7*

Returns an array of usage statistics

int getservbyname(string service, string protocol)   *4.0*

Returns port associated with service; protocol must be "tcp" or "udp"

string getservbyport(int port, string protocol)   *4.0*

Returns service name associated with port; protocol must be "tcp" or "udp"

string gettext(string msgid)   *3.0.7*

Returns the translation of msgid for the current domain or msgid unaltered if a translation does not exist

array gettimeofday(void)   *3.0.7*

Returns the current time as array

string gettype(mixed var)   *3.0*

Returns the type of the variable

array glob(string pattern[, int flags])   *4.3.0*

Finds pathnames matching a pattern

global var1[,var2[, ...]]   *3.0*

Language keyword used inside functions to indicate all uses for specified variables will be global

string gmdate(string format[, int timestamp])   *3.0*

Formats a GMT/UTC date/time

int gmmktime(int hour, int min, int sec, int mon, int day, int year)   *3.0*

Gets Unix timestamp for a GMT date

resource gmp_abs(resource a)   *4.0.4*

Calculates absolute value

resource gmp_add(resource a, resource b)   *4.0.4*
    Adds a and b

resource gmp_and(resource a, resource b)   *4.0.4*
    Calculates logical AND of a and b

void gmp_clrbit(resource &a, int index)   *4.0.4*
    Clears bit in a

int gmp_cmp(resource a, resource b)   *4.0.4*
    Compares two numbers

resource gmp_com(resource a)   *4.0.4*
    Calculates one's complement of a

resource gmp_div_q(resource a, resource b[, int round])   *4.0.4*
    Divides a by b, returns quotient only

array gmp_div_qr(resource a, resource b[, int round])   *4.0.4*
    Divides a by b, returns quotient and reminder

resource gmp_div_r(resource a, resource b[, int round])   *4.0.4*
    Divides a by b, returns reminder only

resource gmp_divexact(resource a, resource b)   *4.0.4*
    Divides a by b using exact division algorithm

resource gmp_fact(int a)   *4.0.4*
    Calculates factorial function

resource gmp_gcd(resource a, resource b)   *4.0.4*
    Computes greatest common denominator (GCD) of a and b

array gmp_gcdext(resource a, resource b)   *4.0.4*
    Computes G, S, and T, such that $AS + BT = G$, where G is the GCD of a and b

int gmp_hamdist(resource a, resource b)   *4.0.4*
    Calculates hamming distance between a and b

resource gmp_init(mixed number[, int base])   *4.0.4*
    Initializes GMP number

int gmp_intval(resource gmpnumber)   *4.0.4*
    Gets signed long value of GMP number

resource gmp_invert(resource a, resource b)   *4.0.4*
    Computes the inverse of a modulo b

int gmp_jacobi(resource a, resource b)   *4.0.4*
    Computes Jacobi symbol

int gmp_legendre(resource a, resource b)   *4.0.4*
    Computes Legendre symbol

resource gmp_mod(resource a, resource b)   *4.0.4*
    Computes a modulo b

resource gmp_mul(resource a, resource b)   *4.0.4*
    Multiplies a and b

resource gmp_neg(resource a)   *4.0.4*
    Negates a number

resource gmp_or(resource a, resource b)   *4.0.4*
    Calculates logical OR of a and b

bool gmp_perfect_square(resource a)   *4.0.4*
    Checks if a is an exact square

int gmp_popcount(resource a)   *4.0.4*
    Calculates the population count of a

resource gmp_pow(resource base, int exp)   *4.0.4*
    Raises base to power exp

resource gmp_powm(resource base, resource exp, resource mod)   *4.0.4*
    Raises base to power exp and takes result modulo mod

int gmp_prob_prime(resource a[, int reps])   *4.0.4*
    Checks if a is "probably prime"

resource gmp_random([int limiter])   *4.0.4*
    Gets random number

int gmp_scan0(resource a, int start)   *4.0.4*
    Finds first zero bit

int gmp_scan1(resource a, int start)   *4.0.4*
    Finds first nonzero bit

void gmp_setbit(resource &a, int index[, bool set_clear]) *4.0.4*
    Sets or clears bit in a

int gmp_sign(resource a)   *4.0.4*
    Gets the sign of the number

resource gmp_sqrt(resource a)   4.0.4
    Takes integer part of square root of a

array gmp_sqrtrem(resource a)   4.0.4
    Takes square root with remainder

string gmp_strval(resource gmpnumber[, int base])   4.0.4
    Gets string representation of GMP number

resource gmp_sub(resource a, resource b)   4.0.4
    Subtracts b from a

resource gmp_xor(resource a, resource b)   4.0.4
    Calculates logical exclusive OR of a and b

string gmstrftime(string format[, int timestamp])   3.0.12
    Formats a GMT/UCT time/date according to locale settings

int gregoriantojd(int month, int day, int year)   3.0
    Converts a Gregorian calendar date to Julian day count

string gzcompress(string data[, int level])   4.0.1
    Gzip-compresses a string

string gzdeflate(string data[, int level])   4.0.4
    Gzip-compresses a string

string gzencode(string data[, int level[, int encoding_mode]])   4.0.4
    Gzip-encodes a string

array gzfile(string filename[, int use_include_path])   3.0
    Reads and uncompresses an entire *.gz* file into an array

string gzinflate(string data[, int length])   4.0.4
    Unzips a gzip-compressed string

int gzopen(string filename, string mode[, int use_include_path])   3.0
    Opens a *.gz* file and returns a *.gz* file pointer

string gzuncompress(string data, int length)   4.0.1
    Unzips a gzip-compressed string

void header(string header[, bool replace, [int http_response_code]])   3.0
    Sends a raw HTTP header

int headers_sent(void)   3.0.8
    Returns true if headers have already been sent, false otherwise

---

string hebrev(string str[, int max_chars_per_line])   *3.0*
    Converts logical Hebrew text to visual text

string hebrevc(string str[, int max_chars_per_line])   *3.0*
    Converts logical Hebrew text to visual text with newline conversion

int hexdec(string hexadecimal_number)   *3.0*
    Returns the decimal equivalent of the hexadecimal number

bool highlight_file(string file_name[, bool return])   *4.0*
    Adds syntax highlighting to a source file

bool highlight_string(string string[, bool return])   *4.0*
    Adds syntax highlighting to a string and optionally return it

string html_entity_decode(string string[, int quote_style][, string charset]) *4.3.0*
    Converts all HTML entities to their applicable characters

string htmlentities(string string[, int quote_style][, string charset])   *3.0*
    Converts all applicable characters to HTML entities

string htmlspecialchars(string string[, int quote_style][, string charset])   *3.0*
    Converts special characters to HTML entities

string iconv(string in_charset, string out_charset, string str)   *4.0.5*
    Returns str converted to the out_charset character set

array iconv_get_encoding([string type])   *4.0.5*
    Gets the internal and output encoding for ob_iconv_handler( )

bool iconv_set_encoding(string type, string charset)   *4.0.5*
    Sets the internal and output encoding for ob_iconv_handler( )

if(cond)   *3.0*
    Language keyword that tests a condition

int ignore_user_abort(bool value)   *3.0.7*
    Sets whether to ignore a user abort event or not

int image2wbmp(int im[, string filename[, int threshold]])   *4.0.5*
    Outputs WBMP image to browser or file

array image_type_to_mime_type(int imagetype)   *4.3.0*
    Gets the MIME type for imagetype returned by getimagesize(), exif_read_data(), exif_thumbnail(), and exif_imagetype()

void imagealphablending(resource im, bool on)   *4.0.6*
    Turns alpha blending mode on or off for the given image

int imagearc(int im, int cx, int cy, int w, int h, int s, int e, int col)   *3.0*
    Draws a partial ellipse

int imagechar(int im, int font, int x, int y, string c, int col)   *3.0*
    Draws a character

int imagecharup(int im, int font, int x, int y, string c, int col)   *3.0*
    Draws a character rotated 90 degrees counterclockwise

int imagecolorallocate(int im, int red, int green, int blue)   *3.0*
    Allocates a color for an image

int imagecolorat(int im, int x, int y)   *3.0*
    Gets the index of the color of a pixel

int imagecolorclosest(int im, int red, int green, int blue)   *3.0*
    Gets the index of the closest color to the specified color

**int imagecolorclosestalpha(resource im, int red, int green, int blue,
int alpha)**   *4.0.6*
    Finds the closest matching color with alpha transparency

int imagecolorclosesthwb(int im, int red, int green, int blue)   *4.0.1*
    Gets the index of the color that has the hue, white, and blackness nearest to the given color

int imagecolordeallocate(int im, int index)   *3.0.6*
    Deallocates a color for an image

int imagecolorexact(int im, int red, int green, int blue)   *3.0*
    Gets the index of the specified color

int imagecolorexactalpha(resource im, int red, int green, int blue, int alpha) *4.0.6*
    Finds exact match for color with transparency

int imagecolorresolve(int im, int red, int green, int blue)   *3.0.2*
    Gets the index of the specified color or its closest possible alternative

**int imagecolorresolvealpha(resource im, int red, int green, int blue,
int alpha)**   *4.0.6*
    Resolves/allocates a color with an alpha level; works for true color and palette based images

---

int imagecolorset(int im, int col, int red, int green, int blue)   *3.0*
    Sets the color for the specified palette index

array imagecolorsforindex(int im, int col)   *3.0*
    Gets the colors for an index

int imagecolorstotal(int im)   *3.0*
    Finds out the number of colors in an image's palette

int imagecolortransparent(int im[, int col])   *3.0*
    Defines a color as transparent

int imagecopy(int dst_im, int src_im, int dst_x, int dst_y, int src_x,
int src_y, int src_w, int src_h)   *3.0.6*
    Copies part of an image

int imagecopymerge(int src_im, int dst_im, int dst_x, int dst_y,
int src_x, int src_y, int src_w, int src_h, int pct)   *4.0.1*
    Merges one part of an image with another

int imagecopymergegray(int src_im, int dst_im, int dst_x, int dst_y,
int src_x, int src_y, int src_w, int src_h, int pct)   *4.0.6*
    Merges one part of an image with another

int imagecopyresampled(int dst_im, int src_im, int dst_x, int dst_y,
int src_x, int src_y, int dst_w, int dst_h, int src_w, int src_h)   *4.0.6*
    Copies and resizes part of an image using resampling to help
    ensure clarity

int imagecopyresized(int dst_im, int src_im, int dst_x, int dst_y,
int src_x, int src_y, int dst_w, int dst_h, int src_w, int src_h)   *3.0*
    Copies and resizes part of an image

int imagecreate(int x_size, int y_size)   *3.0*
    Creates a new image

int imagecreatefromgd(string filename)   *4.1.0*
    Creates a new image from GD file or URL

int imagecreatefromgd2(string filename)   *4.1.0*
    Creates a new image from GD2 file or URL

int imagecreatefromgd2part(string filename, int srcX, int srcY,
int width, int height)   *4.1.0*
    Creates a new image from a given part of GD2 file or URL

int imagecreatefromgif(string filename)   *3.0*
    Creates a new image from GIF file or URL

int imagecreatefromjpeg(string filename) *3.0.16*
  Creates a new image from JPEG file or URL

int imagecreatefrompng(string filename) *3.0.13*
  Creates a new image from PNG file or URL

int imagecreatefromstring(string image) *4.0.4*
  Creates a new image from the image stream in the string

int imagecreatefromwbmp(string filename) *4.0.1*
  Creates a new image from WBMP file or URL

int imagecreatefromxbm(string filename) *4.0.1*
  Creates a new image from XBM file or URL

int imagecreatefromxpm(string filename) *4.0.1*
  Creates a new image from XPM file or URL

int imagecreatetruecolor(int x_size, int y_size) *4.0.6*
  Creates a new true color image

int imagedashedline(int im, int x1, int y1, int x2, int y2, int col) *3.0*
  Draws a dashed line

int imagedestroy(int im) *3.0*
  Destroys an image

void imageellipse(resource im, int cx, int cy, int w, int h, int color) *4.0.6*
  Draws an ellipse

int imagefill(int im, int x, int y, int col) *3.0*
  Performs a flood fill

int imagefilledarc(int im, int cx, int cy, int w, int h, int s, int e, int col, int style) *4.0.6*
  Draws a filled partial ellipse

void imagefilledellipse(resource im, int cx, int cy, int w, int h, int color) *4.0.6*
  Draws an ellipse

int imagefilledpolygon(int im, array point, int num_points, int col) *3.0*
  Draws a filled polygon

int imagefilledrectangle(int im, int x1, int y1, int x2, int y2, int col) *3.0*
  Draws a filled rectangle

int imagefilltoborder(int im, int x, int y, int border, int col) *3.0*
  Performs a flood fill to specific color

int imagefontheight(int font) _3.0_
    Gets font height

int imagefontwidth(int font) _3.0_
    Gets font width

array imageftbbox(int size, int angle, string font_file, string text[, array extrainfo]) _4.1.0_
    Gives the bounding box of a text using fonts via freetype2

array imagefttext(int im, int size, int angle, int x, int y, int col, string font_file, string text, [array extrainfo]) _4.1.0_
    Writes text to the image using fonts via freetype2

int imagegammacorrect(int im, float inputgamma, float outputgamma) _3.0.13_
    Applies a gamma correction to a GD image

int imagegd(int im[, string filename]) _4.1.0_
    Outputs GD image to browser or file

int imagegd2(int im[, string filename]) _4.1.0_
    Outputs GD2 image to browser or file

int imagegif(int im[, string filename]) _3.0_
    Outputs GIF image to browser or file

int imageinterlace(int im[, int interlace]) _3.0_
    Enables or disables interlace

int imagejpeg(int im[, string filename[, int quality]]) _3.0.16_
    Outputs JPEG image to browser or file

int imageline(int im, int x1, int y1, int x2, int y2, int col) _3.0_
    Draws a line

int imageloadfont(string filename) _3.0_
    Loads a new font

int imagepalettecopy(int dst, int src) _4.0.1_
    Copies the palette from the src image onto the dst image

int imagepng(int im[, string filename]) _3.0.13_
    Outputs PNG image to browser or file

int imagepolygon(int im, array point, int num_points, int col) _3.0_
    Draws a polygon

array imagepsbbox(string text, int font, int size[, int space,
int tightness, int angle]) *3.0.9*
    Returns the bounding box needed by a string if rasterized

int imagepscopyfont(int font_index) *3.0.9*
    Makes a copy of a font for purposes like extending or reencoding

bool imagepsencodefont(int font_index, string filename) *3.0.9*
    Changes a font's character encoding vector

bool imagepsextendfont(int font_index, float extend) *3.0.9*
    Extends or condenses (if extend is less than 1) a font

bool imagepsfreefont(int font_index) *3.0.9*
    Frees memory used by a font

int imagepsloadfont(string pathname) *3.0.9*
    Loads a new font from specified file

bool imagepsslantfont(int font_index, float slant) *3.0.9*
    Slants a font

array imagepstext(int image, string text, int font, int size, int xcoord,
int ycoord[, int space, int tightness, float angle, int antialias]) *3.0.9*
    Rasterizes a string over an image

int imagerectangle(int im, int x1, int y1, int x2, int y2, int col) *3.0*
    Draws a rectangle

int imagesetbrush(resource image, resource brush) *4.0.6*
    Sets the brush image for line drawing

int imagesetpixel(int im, int x, int y, int col) *3.0*
    Sets a single pixel

void imagesetstyle(resource im, array styles) *4.0.6*
    Sets the style for line drawing

void imagesetthickness(resource im, int thickness) *4.0.6*
    Sets line thickness for line drawing

int imagesettile(resource image, resource tile) *4.0.6*
    Sets the tile image for filling

int imagestring(int im, int font, int x, int y, string str, int col) *3.0*
    Draws a string horizontally

---

int imagestringup(int im, int font, int x, int y, string str, int col)   *3.0*
    Draws a string vertically (rotated 90 degrees counterclockwise)

int imagesx(int im)   *3.0*
    Gets image width

int imagesy(int im)   *3.0*
    Gets image height

void imagetruecolortopalette(resource im, bool ditherFlag, int colorsWanted)   *4.0.6*
    Converts a true color image to a palette-based image with a number of colors, optionally using dithering.

array imagettfbbox(int size, int angle, string font_file, string text)   *3.0.1*
    Gives the bounding box of a text using TrueType fonts

array imagettftext(int im, int size, int angle, int x, int y, int col, string font_file, string text)   *3.0*
    Writes text to the image using a TrueType font

int imagetypes(void)   *3 CVS Only*
    Returns the types of images supported in a bitfield (1=GIF, 2=JPEG, 4=PNG, 8=WBMP, 16=XPM)

int imagewbmp(int im[, string filename,[, int foreground]])   *3.0.15*
    Outputs WBMP image to browser or file

string imap_8bit(string text)   *3.0*
    Converts an 8-bit string to a quoted-printable string

array imap_alerts(void)   *3.0.12*
    Returns an array of all IMAP alerts generated since the last page load or the last imap_alerts() call, whichever came last, and clears the alert stack

int imap_append(int stream_id, string folder, string message[, string flags])   *3.0*
    Appends a new message to a specified mailbox

string imap_base64(string text)   *3.0*
    Decodes BASE64 encoded text

string imap_binary(string text)   *3.0.2*
    Converts an 8-bit string to a base64 string

string imap_body(int stream_id, int msg_no[, int options])   *3.0*
    Reads the message body

object imap_bodystruct(int stream_id, int msg_no, int section) *3.0.4*
Reads the structure of a specified body section of a specific message

object imap_check(int stream_id) *3.0*
Gets mailbox properties

int imap_clearflag_full(int stream_id, string sequence, string flag[, int options]) *3.0.3*
Clears flags on messages

int imap_close(int stream_id[, int options]) *3.0*
Closes an IMAP stream

int imap_createmailbox(int stream_id, string mailbox) *3.0*
Creates a new mailbox

int imap_delete(int stream_id, int msg_no[, int flags]) *3.0*
Marks a message for deletion

int imap_deletemailbox(int stream_id, string mailbox) *3.0*
Deletes a mailbox

array imap_errors(void) *3.0.12*
Returns an array of all IMAP errors generated since the last page load or the last imap_errors( ) call, whichever came last, and clears the error stack

int imap_expunge(int stream_id) *3.0*
Permanently deletes all messages marked for deletion

array imap_fetch_overview(int stream_id, int msg_no[, int flags]) *3.0.4*
Reads an overview of the information in the headers of the given message sequence

string imap_fetchbody(int stream_id, int msg_no, int section[, int options]) *3.0*
Gets a specific body section

string imap_fetchheader(int stream_id, int msg_no[, int options]) *3.0.3*
Gets the full unfiltered header for a message

object imap_fetchstructure(int stream_id, int msg_no[, int options]) *3.0*
Reads the full structure of a message

array imap_get_quota(int stream_id, string qroot) *4.0.5*
Returns the quota set to the mailbox account qroot

array imap_get_quotaroot(int stream_id, string mbox)   *4.3.0*
    Returns the quota set to the mailbox account mbox

array imap_getmailboxes(int stream_id, string ref, string pattern)   *3.0.12*
    Reads the list of mailboxes and returns a full array of objects
    containing names, attributes, and delimiters

array imap_getsubscribed(int stream_id, string ref, string pattern)   *3.0.12*
    Return a list of subscribed mailboxes in the same format as
    imap_getmailboxes( )

object imap_headerinfo(int stream_id, int msg_no[, int from_length[,
int subject_length[, string default_host]]])   *3.0*
    Reads the headers of the message

array imap_headers(int stream_id)   *3.0*
    Returns headers for all messages in a mailbox

string imap_last_error(void)   *3.0.12*
    Returns the last error that was generated by an IMAP func-
    tion; the error stack is not cleared after this call

array imap_list(int stream_id, string ref, string pattern)   *3.0.4*
    Reads the list of mailboxes

array imap_lsub(int stream_id, string ref, string pattern)   *3.0.4*
    Returns a list of subscribed mailboxes

int imap_mail(string to, string subject, string message[, string
additional_headers[, string cc[, string bcc[, string rpath]]]])   *3.0.14*
    Sends an email message

string imap_mail_compose(array envelope, array body)   *3.0.5*
    Creates a MIME message based on given envelope and body
    sections

int imap_mail_copy(int stream_id, int msg_no, string mailbox[,
int options])   *3.0*
    Copies specified message to a mailbox

int imap_mail_move(int stream_id, int msg_no, string mailbox[,
int options])   *3.0*
    Moves specified message to a mailbox

object imap_mailboxmsginfo(int stream_id)   *3.0.2*
    Returns information about the current mailbox

array imap_mime_header_decode(string str) *3.0.17*
    Decodes MIME header element in accordance with RFC 2047 and returns an array of objects containing charset encoding and decoded text

int imap_msgno(int stream_id, int unique_msg_id) *3.0.3*
    Gets the sequence number associated with a user ID

int imap_num_msg(int stream_id) *3.0*
    Gives the number of messages in the current mailbox

int imap_num_recent(int stream_id) *3.0*
    Gives the number of recent messages in current mailbox

int imap_open(string mailbox, string user, string password[, int options]) *3.0*
    Opens an IMAP stream to a mailbox

int imap_ping(int stream_id) *3.0*
    Checks if the IMAP stream is still active

string imap_qprint(string text) *3.0*
    Converts a quoted-printable string to an 8-bit string

int imap_renamemailbox(int stream_id, string old_name, string new_name) *3.0*
    Renames a mailbox

int imap_reopen(int stream_id, string mailbox[, int options]) *3.0*
    Reopens an IMAP stream to a new mailbox

array imap_rfc822_parse_adrlist(string address_string, string default_host) *3.0.2*
    Parses an address string

object imap_rfc822_parse_headers(string headers[, string default_host]) *4.0*
    Parses a set of mail headers contained in a string and return an object similar to `imap_headerinfo()`

string imap_rfc822_write_address(string mailbox, string host, string personal) *3.0.2*
    Returns a properly formatted email address given the mailbox, host, and personal information

array imap_scan(int stream_id, string ref, string pattern, string content) *3.0.4*
    Reads list of mailboxes containing a certain string

array imap_search(int stream_id, string criteria[, long flags]) *3.0.12*
    Returns a list of messages matching the given criteria

int imap_set_quota(int stream_id, string qroot, int mailbox_size)   *4.0.5*
    Sets the quota for qroot mailbox

int imap_setacl(int stream_id, string mailbox, string id, string rights)   *4.1.0*
    Sets the ACL for a given mailbox

**int imap_setflag_full(int stream_id, string sequence, string flag[,
int options])**   *3.0.3*
    Sets flags on messages

**array imap_sort(int stream_id, int criteria, int reverse[, int options[,
string search_criteria]])**   *3.0.3*
    Sorts an array of message headers, optionally including only
    messages that meet specified criteria

object imap_status(int stream_id, string mailbox, int options)   *3.0.4*
    Gets status information from a mailbox

int imap_subscribe(int stream_id, string mailbox)   *3.0*
    Subscribes to a mailbox

int imap_thread(int stream_id[, int flags])   *4.1.0*
    Returns threaded by references tree

int imap_uid(int stream_id, int msg_no)   *3.0.3*
    Gets the unique message ID associated with a standard
    sequential message number

int imap_undelete(int stream_id, int msg_no)   *3.0*
    Removes the delete flag from a message

int imap_unsubscribe(int stream_id, string mailbox)   *3.0*
    Unsubscribes from a mailbox

string imap_utf7_decode(string buf)   *3.0.15*
    Decodes a modified UTF-7 string

string imap_utf7_encode(string buf)   *3.0.15*
    Encodes a string in modified UTF-7

string imap_utf8(string string)   *3.0.13*
    Converts a string to UTF-8

string implode(array src, string glue)   *3.0*
    Joins array elements placing glue string between items and
    returns one string

bool import_request_variables(string types[, string prefix])   *4.1.0*
    Imports GET/POST/Cookie variables into the global scope

bool in_array(mixed needle, array haystack[, bool strict])   *4.0*
    Checks if the given value exists in the array

bool include filename   *3.0*
    Includes and evaluates the given file, with a nonfatal warning on failure

bool include_once filename   *4.0*
    Includes and evaluates the given file if not already included, with a nonfatal warning on failure

string ini_get(string varname)   *4.0*
    Gets a configuration option

array ini_get_all([string extension])   *4.1.0*
    Gets all configuration options

string ini_restore(string varname)   *4.0*
    Restores the value of a configuration option specified by varname

string ini_set(string varname, string newvalue)   *4.0*
    Sets a configuration option; returns false on error and the old value of the configuration option on success

int intval(mixed var[, int base])   *3.0*
    Gets the integer value of a variable using the optional base for the conversion

int ip2long(string ip_address)   *4.0*
    Converts a string containing an (IPv4) Internet Protocol dotted address into a proper address

array iptcembed(string iptcdata, string jpeg_file_name[, int spool])   *3.0.7*
    Embeds binary IPTC data into a JPEG image.

array iptcparse(string iptcdata)   *3.0.6*
    Parses binary IPTC data into associative array

bool is_a(object object, string class_name)   *4.1.0*
    Returns true if the object is of this class or has this class as one of its parents

bool is_array(mixed var)   *3.0*
    Returns true if variable is an array

---

bool is_bool(mixed var)	*4.0*
Returns true if variable is a boolean	
bool is_callable(mixed var[, bool syntax_only[, string callable_name]])	*4.0.6*
Returns true if variable is callable	
bool is_dir(string filename)	*3.0*
Returns true if file is directory	
bool is_executable(string filename)	*3.0*
Returns true if file is executable	
bool is_file(string filename)	*3.0*
Returns true if file is a regular file	
bool is_finite(float val)	*4.1.0*
Returns whether argument is finite	
bool is_float(mixed var)	*3.0*
Returns true if variable is float point	
bool is_infinite(float val)	*4.1.0*
Returns whether argument is infinite	
bool is_link(string filename)	*3.0*
Returns true if file is symbolic link	
bool is_long(mixed var)	*3.0*
Returns true if variable is a long (integer)	
bool is_nan(float val)	*4.1.0*
Returns whether argument is not a number	
bool is_null(mixed var)	*4.0.4*
Returns true if variable is NULL	
bool is_numeric(mixed value)	*4.0*
Returns true if value is a number or a numeric string	
bool is_object(mixed var)	*3.0*
Returns true if variable is an object	
bool is_readable(string filename)	*3.0*
Returns true if file can be read	
bool is_resource(mixed var)	*4.0*
Returns true if variable is a resource	

bool is_scalar(mixed value) *4.0.5*
    Returns true if value is a scalar

bool is_string(mixed var) *3.0*
    Returns true if variable is a string

bool is_subclass_of(object object, string class_name) *4.0*
    Returns true if the object has this class as one of its parents

bool is_uploaded_file(string path) *3.0.17*
    Checks if file was created by RFC 1867 upload

bool is_writable(string filename) *4.0*
    Returns true if file can be written

bool isset(mixed var[, mixed var[, ...]]) *3.0*
    Determines whether a variable is set

void java_last_exception_clear(void) *4.0.2*
    Clears last Java extension

object java_last_exception_get(void) *4.0.2*
    Gets last Java exception

mixed jddayofweek(int juliandaycount[, int mode]) *3.0*
    Returns name or number of day of week from Julian day count

string jdmonthname(int juliandaycount, int mode) *3.0*
    Returns name of month for Julian day count

string jdtofrench(int juliandaycount) *3.0*
    Converts a Julian day count to a French Republic calendar date

string jdtogregorian(int juliandaycount) *3.0*
    Converts a Julian day count to a Gregorian calendar date

string jdtojewish(int juliandaycount) *3.0*
    Converts a Julian day count to a Jewish calendar date

string jdtojulian(int juliandaycount) *3.0*
    Converts a Julian day count to a Julian calendar date

int jdtounix(int jday) *4.0*
    Convert Julian day count to a Unix timestamp

int jewishtojd(int month, int day, int year) *3.0*
    Converts a Jewish calendar date to a Julian day count

---

string join(array src, string glue)   *3.0*
  An alias for `implode()`

void jpeg2wbmp (string f_org, string f_dest, int d_height,
int d_width, int threshold)   *4.0.5*
  Converts JPEG image to WBMP image

int juliantojd(int month, int day, int year)   *3.0*
  Converts a Julian calendar date to a Julian day count

mixed key(array array_arg)   *3.0*
  Returns the key of the element currently pointed to by the
  internal array pointer

bool krsort(array array_arg[, int sort_flags])   *3.0.13*
  Sorts an array by key value in reverse order

bool ksort(array array_arg[, int sort_flags])   *3.0*
  Sorts an array by key

float lcg_value()   *4.0*
  Returns a value from the combined linear congruential
  generator

string ldap_8859_to_t61(string value)   *4.0.2*
  Translates 8859 characters to t61 characters

bool ldap_add(resource link, string dn, array entry)   *3.0*
  Adds entries to an LDAP directory

bool ldap_bind(resource link[, string dn, string password])   *3.0*
  Binds to an LDAP directory

bool ldap_compare(resource link, string dn, string attr, string value)   *4.0.2*
  Determines if an entry has a specific value for one of its
  attributes

resource ldap_connect([string host[, int port]])   *3.0*
  Connects to an LDAP server

int ldap_count_entries(resource link, resource result)   *3.0*
  Counts the number of entries in a search result

bool ldap_delete(resource link, string dn)   *3.0*
  Deletes an entry from a directory

string ldap_dn2ufn(string dn)   *3.0*
  Converts DN to User Friendly Naming format

---

string ldap_err2str(int errno)   *3.0.13*
    Converts error number to error string

int ldap_errno(resource link)   *3.0.12*
    Gets the current LDAP error number

string ldap_error(resource link)   *3.0.12*
    Gets the current LDAP error string

array ldap_explode_dn(string dn, int with_attrib)   *3.0*
    Splits DN into its component parts

string ldap_first_attribute(resource link, resource result_entry, int ber)   *3.0*
    Returns first attribute

resource ldap_first_entry(resource link, resource result)   *3.0*
    Returns first result ID

resource ldap_first_reference(resource link, resource result)   *4.0.5*
    Returns first reference

bool ldap_free_result(resource result)   *3.0*
    Frees result memory

array ldap_get_attributes(resource link, resource result_entry)   *3.0*
    Gets attributes from a search result entry

string ldap_get_dn(resource link, resource result_entry)   *3.0*
    Gets the DN of a result entry

array ldap_get_entries(resource link, resource result)   *3.0*
    Gets all result entries

bool ldap_get_option(resource link, int option, mixed retval)   *4.0.4*
    Gets the current value of various session-wide parameters

array ldap_get_values(resource link, resource result_entry, string attribute)   *3.0*
    Gets all values from a result entry

array ldap_get_values_len(resource link, resource result_entry, string attribute)   *3.0.13*
    Gets all values with lengths from a result entry

resource ldap_list(resource link, string base_dn, string filter[, array attrs[, int attrsonly[, int sizelimit[, int timelimit[, int deref]]]]])   *3.0*
    Performs a single-level search

bool ldap_mod_add(resource link, string dn, array entry)   *3.0.8*
    Adds attribute values to current

bool ldap_mod_del(resource link, string dn, array entry)   *3.0.8*
    Deletes attribute values

bool ldap_mod_replace(resource link, string dn, array entry)   *3.0.8*
    Replaces attribute values with new ones

string ldap_next_attribute(resource link, resource result_entry, resource ber)   *3.0*
    Gets the next attribute in result

resource ldap_next_entry(resource link, resource result_entry)   *3.0*
    Gets next result entry

resource ldap_next_reference(resource link, resource reference_entry)   *4.0.5*
    Gets next reference

bool ldap_parse_reference(resource link, resource reference_entry, array referrals)   *4.0.5*
    Extracts information from reference entry

bool ldap_parse_result(resource link, resource result, int errcode, string matcheddn, string errmsg, array referrals)   *4.0.5*
    Extracts information from result

resource ldap_read(resource link, string base_dn, string filter[, array attrs[, int attrsonly[, int sizelimit[, int timelimit[, int deref]]]]])   *3.0*
    Reads an entry

bool ldap_rename(resource link, string dn, string newrdn, string newparent, bool deleteoldrdn);   *4.0.5*
    Modifies the name of an entry

resource ldap_search(resource link, string base_dn, string filter[, array attrs[, int attrsonly[, int sizelimit[, int timelimit[, int deref]]]]])   *3.0*
    Searches LDAP tree under base_dn

bool ldap_set_option(resource link, int option, mixed newval)   *4.0.4*
    Set the value of various session-wide parameters

bool ldap_set_rebind_proc(resource link, string callback)   *4.1.0*
    Sets a callback function to do rebinds on referral chasing

bool ldap_sort(resource link, resource result, string sortfilter)   *4.1.0*
    Sorts LDAP result entries

bool ldap_start_tls(resource link)   *4.1.0*
    Starts TLS

string ldap_t61_to_8859(string value) *4.0.2*
Translates t61 characters to 8859 characters

bool ldap_unbind(resource link) *3.0*
Unbinds from LDAP directory

void leak(int num_bytes=3) *3.0*
Causes an intentional memory leak for testing/debugging purposes

int levenshtein(string str1, string str2) *3.0.17*
Calculates Levenshtein distance between two strings

int link(string target, string link) *3.0*
Creates a hard link

int linkinfo(string filename) *3.0*
Returns the st_dev field of the Unix C stat structure describing the link

void list(mixed var[, mixed var[, ...]]) *3.0*
Assigns variables as if they were an array

array localeconv(void) *4.0.5*
Returns numeric formatting information based on the current locale

array localtime([int timestamp[, bool associative_array]]) *4.0*
Returns the results of the C system call localtime as an associative array if the associative_array argument is set to 1 or as a regular array

float log(float number) *3.0*
Returns the natural logarithm of the number

float log10(float number) *3.0*
Returns the base-10 logarithm of the number

float log1p(float number) *4.1.0*
Returns log(1 + number), computed in a way that is accurate even when the value of number is close to zero

string long2ip(int proper_address) *4.0*
Converts an (IPv4) Internet network address into a string in Internet standard dotted format

array lstat(string filename) *3.0.4*
Gives information about a file or symbolic link

---

string ltrim(string str[, string character_mask]) *3.0*
    Strips whitespace from the beginning of a string

int mail(string to, string subject, string message[, string additional_headers[, string additional_parameters]]) *3.0*
    Sends an email message

mixed max(mixed arg1[, mixed arg2[, mixed ...]]) *3.0*
    Return the highest value in an array or a series of arguments

string mb_convert_encoding(string str, string to-encoding[, mixed from-encoding]) *4.0.6*
    Returns converted string in desired encoding

string mb_convert_kana(string str[, string option][, string encoding]) *4.0.6*
    Converts between full-width characters and half-width characters (Japanese)

string mb_convert_variables(string to-encoding, mixed from-encoding, mixed vars[, mixed ...]) *4.0.6*
    Converts the string resource(s) in variable(s) to desired encoding

string mb_decode_mimeheader(string string) *4.0.6*
    Decodes encoded-word string in MIME header field

string mb_decode_numericentity(string string, array convmap[, string encoding]) *4.0.6*
    Converts HTML numeric entities to character codes

string mb_detect_encoding(string str[, mixed encoding_list]) *4.0.6*
    Returns encoding of the given string

bool|array mb_detect_order([mixed encoding-list]) *4.0.6*
    Sets the current detect_order or returns the current detect_order as an array

string mb_encode_mimeheader(string str[, string charset[, string transfer-encoding[, string linefeed]]]) *4.0.6*
    Converts the string to a MIME encoded-word in the format of =?charset?(B|Q)?encoded_string?=

string mb_encode_numericentity(string string, array convmap[, string encoding]) *4.0.6*
    Converts specified characters to HTML numeric entities

string mb_get_info([string type])   *4.1.0*
  Returns the current settings of mbstring

false|string mb_http_input([string type])   *4.0.6*
  Returns the input encoding

string mb_http_output([string encoding])   *4.0.6*
  Sets the current output_encoding or returns the current
  output_encoding as a string

string mb_internal_encoding([string encoding])   *4.0.6*
  Sets the current internal encoding or returns the current
  internal encoding as a string

string mb_language([string language])   *4.0.6*
  Sets the current language or returns the current language as a
  string

string mb_output_handler(string contents, int status)   *4.0.6*
  Returns string in output buffer converted to the http_output
  encoding

bool mb_parse_str(string encoded_string[, array result])   *4.0.6*
  Parses GET/POST/Cookie data and sets global variables

string mb_preferred_mime_name(string encoding)   *4.0.6*
  Returns the preferred MIME name (charset) as a string

int mb_send_mail(string to, string subject, string message[, string
additional_headers[, string additional_parameters]])   *4.0.6*
  Sends an email message with MIME scheme

string mb_strcut(string str, int start[, int length[, string encoding]])   *4.0.6*
  Returns part of a string

string mb_strimwidth(string str, int start, int width[, string trimmarker[,
string encoding]])   *4.0.6*
  Trims the string in terminal width

int mb_strlen(string str[, string encoding])   *4.0.6*
  Gets character numbers of a string

int mb_strpos(string haystack, string needle[, int offset[, string encoding]])   *4.0.6*
  Finds position of first occurrence of a string within another

int mb_strrpos(string haystack, string needle[, string encoding])   *4.0.6*
  Finds the last occurrence of a character in a string within
  another

---

int mb_strwidth(string str[, string encoding])   *4.0.6*
    Gets terminal width of a string

mixed mb_substitute_character([mixed substchar])   *4.0.6*
    Sets the current substitute_character or returns the current
    substitute_character

string mb_substr(string str, int start[, int length[, string encoding]])   *4.0.6*
    Returns part of a string

string mcrypt_cbc(int cipher, string key, string data, int mode[, string iv])   *3.0.8*
    CBC encrypts/decrypts data using key with cipher starting
    with optional iv

string mcrypt_cfb(int cipher, string key, string data, int mode[, string iv])   *3.0.8*
    CFB encrypts/decrypts data using key with cipher starting
    with optional iv

string mcrypt_create_iv(int size, int source)   *3.0.8*
    Creates an initialization vector (IV)

string mcrypt_decrypt(string cipher, string key, string data, string mode[,
string iv])   *4.0.2*
    OFB encrypts/decrypts data using key with cipher starting
    with optional iv

string mcrypt_ecb(int cipher, string key, string data, int mode[, string iv])   *3.0.8*
    ECB encrypts/decrypts data using key with cipher starting
    with optional iv

string mcrypt_enc_get_algorithms_name(resource td)   *4.0.2*
    Returns the name of the algorithm specified by the descriptor
    td

int mcrypt_enc_get_block_size(resource td)   *4.0.2*
    Returns the block size of the cipher specified by the descriptor
    td

int mcrypt_enc_get_iv_size(resource td)   *4.0.2*
    Returns the size of the IV in bytes of the algorithm specified
    by the descriptor td

int mcrypt_enc_get_key_size(resource td)   *4.0.2*
    Returns the maximum supported key size in bytes of the algo-
    rithm specified by the descriptor td

string mcrypt_enc_get_modes_name(resource td)   *4.0.2*
> Returns the name of the mode specified by the descriptor td

int mcrypt_enc_get_supported_key_sizes(resource td)   *4.0.2*
> Returns an array with the supported key sizes of the algorithm specified by the descriptor td

bool mcrypt_enc_is_block_algorithm(resource td)   *4.0.2*
> Returns true if the algorithm is a block algorithm

bool mcrypt_enc_is_block_algorithm_mode(resource td)   *4.0.2*
> Returns true if the mode is for use with block algorithms

bool mcrypt_enc_is_block_mode(resource td)   *4.0.2*
> Returns true if the mode outputs blocks of bytes

int mcrypt_enc_self_test(resource td)   *4.0.2*
> Runs the self test on the algorithm specified by the descriptor td

string mcrypt_encrypt(string cipher, string key, string data, string mode, string iv)   *4.0.2*
> OFB encrypts/decrypts data using key with cipher starting with iv

string mcrypt_generic(resource td, string data)   *4.0.2*
> Encrypts plain text with given parameters

bool mcrypt_generic_deinit(resource td)   *4.1.0*
> Terminates encryption specified by the descriptor td

bool mcrypt_generic_end(resource td)   *4.0.2*
> Terminates encryption specified by the descriptor td

int mcrypt_generic_init(resource td, string key, string iv)   *4.0.2*
> Initializes all buffers for the specific module

int mcrypt_get_block_size(int cipher)   *3.0.8*
> Gets the block size of cipher

int mcrypt_get_block_size(string cipher, string module)   *3.0.8*
> Gets the key size of cipher

string mcrypt_get_cipher_name(string cipher)   *3.0.8*
> Gets the key size of cipher

string mcrypt_get_cipher_name(int cipher)   *3.0.8*
> Gets the name of cipher

---

int mcrypt_get_iv_size(string cipher, string module) *4.0.2*
  Get the IV size of cipher (usually the same as the block size)

int mcrypt_get_key_size(string cipher, string module) *3.0.8*
  Gets the key size of cipher

int mcrypt_get_key_size(int cipher) *3.0.8*
  Gets the key size of cipher

array mcrypt_list_algorithms([string lib_dir]) *4.0.2*
  Lists all supported algorithms

array mcrypt_list_modes([string lib_dir]) *4.0.2*
  Lists all supported modes

bool mcrypt_module_close(resource td) *4.0.2*
  Frees the descriptor td

int mcrypt_module_get_algo_block_size(string algorithm[, string lib_dir]) *4.0.2*
  Returns the block size of the algorithm

int mcrypt_module_get_algo_key_size(string algorithm[, string lib_dir]) *4.0.2*
  Returns the maximum supported key size of the algorithm

int mcrypt_module_get_supported_key_sizes(string algorithm[, string lib_dir]) *4.0.2*
  Returns an array with the supported key sizes of the algorithm

bool mcrypt_module_is_block_algorithm(string algorithm[, string lib_dir]) *4.0.2*
  Returns true if the algorithm is a block algorithm

bool mcrypt_module_is_block_algorithm_mode(string mode[, string lib_dir]) *4.0.2*
  Returns true if the mode is for use with block algorithms

bool mcrypt_module_is_block_mode(string mode[, string lib_dir]) *4.0.2*
  Returns true if the mode outputs blocks of bytes

resource mcrypt_module_open(string cipher, string cipher_directory, string mode, string mode_directory) *4.0.2*
  Opens the module of the algorithm and the mode to be used

bool mcrypt_module_self_test(string algorithm[, string lib_dir]) *4.0.2*
  Does a self test of the specified module

string mcrypt_ofb(int cipher, string key, string data, int mode[, string iv])   *3.0.8*
> OFB encrypts/decrypts data using key with cipher starting with optional iv

string md5(string str)   *3.0*
> Calculates the md5 hash of a string

string md5_file(string filename)   *4.1.0*
> Calculates the md5 hash of given filename

string mdecrypt_generic(resource td, string data)   *4.0.2*
> Decrypts plain text with given parameters

string metaphone(string text, int phones)   *4.0*
> Breaks English phrases down into their phonemes

bool method_exists(object object, string method)   *4.0*
> Checks if the class method exists

string mhash(int hash, string data[, string key])   *3.0.9*
> Hashes data with hash

int mhash_count(void)   *3.0.9*
> Gets the number of available hashes

int mhash_get_block_size(int hash)   *3.0.9*
> Gets the block size of hash

string mhash_get_hash_name(int hash)   *3.0.9*
> Gets the name of hash

string mhash_keygen_s2k(int hash, string input_password, string salt, int bytes)   *4.0.4*
> Generates a key using hash functions

string microtime(void)   *3.0*
> Returns a string containing the current time in seconds and microseconds

string mime_content_type(string filename)   *4.3.0*
> Returns MIME Content-type for file

mixed min(mixed arg1[, mixed arg2[, mixed ...]])   *3.0*
> Returns the lowest value in an array or a series of arguments

bool mkdir(string pathname[, int mode])   *3.0*
> Creates a directory

---

int mktime(int hour, int min, int sec, int mon, int day, int year)   *3.0*
    Gets Unix timestamp for a date

string money_format(string format, float value)   *4.3.0*
    Converts monetary value(s) to string

bool move_uploaded_file(string path, string new_path)   *4.0.3*
    Moves a file if and only if it was created by an upload

resource msg_get_queue(long key[, long perms])   *4.3.0*
    Attaches to a message queue

mixed msg_receive(resource queue, long desiredmsgtype, long &msgtype, long maxsize, mixed message [[, bool unserialize=true][, long flags=0[, long errorcode]]]   *4.3.0*
    Sends a message of type msgtype (must be greater than 0) to a message queue

bool msg_remove_queue(resource queue)   *4.3.0*
    Destroys the queue

bool msg_send(resource queue, long msgtype, mixed message [[, bool serialize=true][, bool blocking=true][, long errorcode]])   *4.3.0*
    Sends a message of type msgtype (must be greater than 0) to a message queue

array msg_set_queue(resource queue, array data)   *4.3.0*
    Sets information for a message queue

array msg_stat_queue(resource queue)   *4.3.0*
    Returns information about a message queue

int mt_getrandmax(void)   *3.0.6*
    Returns the maximum value a random number from Mersenne Twister can have

int mt_rand([int min, int max])   *3.0.6*
    Returns a random number from Mersenne Twister

void mt_srand([int seed])   *3.0.6*
    Seeds Mersenne Twister random number generator

int mysql_affected_rows([int link_identifier])   *3.0*
    Gets number of affected rows in previous MySQL operation

string mysql_character_set_name([int link_identifier])   *4.3.0*
    Returns the default character set for the current connection

bool mysql_close([int link_identifier])   3.0
    Closes a MySQL connection

resource mysql_connect([string hostname[:port][:/path/to/socket]][, string
username[, string password[, bool new[, int flags]]]]])   3.0
    Opens a connection to a MySQL server

bool mysql_create_db(string database_name[, int link_identifier])   3.0
    Creates a MySQL database

bool mysql_data_seek(int result, int row_number)   3.0
    Moves internal result pointer

resource mysql_db_query(string database_name, string query[,
int link_identifier])   3.0
    Sends an SQL query to a MySQL database

bool mysql_drop_db(string database_name[, int link_identifier])   3.0
    Drops (deletes) a MySQL database

int mysql_errno([int link_identifier])   3.0
    Returns the number of the error message from previous
    MySQL operation

string mysql_error([int link_identifier])   3.0
    Returns the text of the error message from previous MySQL
    operation

string mysql_escape_string(string to_be_escaped)   4.0.3
    Escapes string for MySQL query

array mysql_fetch_array(int result[, int result_type])   3.0
    Fetches a result row as an array (associative, numeric, or
    both)

array mysql_fetch_assoc(int result)   4.0.3
    Fetches a result row as an associative array

object mysql_fetch_field(int result[, int field_offset])   3.0
    Gets column information from a result and returns it as an
    object

array mysql_fetch_lengths(int result)   3.0
    Gets maximum data size of each column in a result

object mysql_fetch_object(int result[, int result_type])   3.0
    Fetches a result row as an object

array mysql_fetch_row(int result)   *3.0*
    Gets a result row as an enumerated array

string mysql_field_flags(int result, int field_offset)   *3.0*
    Gets the flags associated with the specified field in a result

int mysql_field_len(int result, int field_offset)   *3.0*
    Returns the length of the specified field

string mysql_field_name(int result, int field_index)   *3.0*
    Gets the name of the specified field in a result

bool mysql_field_seek(int result, int field_offset)   *3.0*
    Sets result pointer to a specific field offset

string mysql_field_table(int result, int field_offset)   *3.0*
    Gets name of the table the specified field is in

string mysql_field_type(int result, int field_offset)   *3.0*
    Gets the type of the specified field in a result

bool mysql_free_result(int result)   *3.0*
    Frees result memory

string mysql_get_client_info(void)   *4.0.5*
    Returns a string that represents the client library version

string mysql_get_host_info([int link_identifier])   *4.0.5*
    Returns a string describing the type of connection in use, including the server host name

int mysql_get_proto_info([int link_identifier])   *4.0.5*
    Returns the protocol version used by current connection

string mysql_get_server_info([int link_identifier])   *4.0.5*
    Returns a string that represents the server version number

string mysql_info([int link_identifier])   *4.3.0*
    Returns a string containing information about the most recent query

int mysql_insert_id([int link_identifier])   *3.0*
    Gets the ID generated from the previous INSERT operation

resource mysql_list_dbs([int link_identifier])   *3.0*
    Lists databases available on a MySQL server

resource mysql_list_fields(string database_name, string table_name[, int link_identifier]) 3.0
    Lists MySQL result fields

resource mysql_list_processes([int link_identifier]) 4.3.0
    Returns a result set describing the current server threads

resource mysql_list_tables(string database_name[, int link_identifier]) 3.0
    Lists tables in a MySQL database

int mysql_num_fields(int result) 3.0
    Gets number of fields in a result

int mysql_num_rows(int result) 3.0
    Gets number of rows in a result

resource mysql_pconnect([string hostname[:port][:/path/to/socket][, string username[, string password[, int flags]]]]) 3.0
    Opens a persistent connection to a MySQL server

bool mysql_ping([int link_identifier]) 4.3.0
    Pings a server connection or reconnects if there is no connection

resource mysql_query(string query[, int link_identifier][, int result_mode]) 3.0
    Sends an SQL query to a MySQL database

string mysql_real_escape_string(string to_be_escaped[, int link_identifier]) 4.3.0
    Escapes special characters in a string for use in a SQL statement, taking into account the current charset of the connection

mixed mysql_result(int result, int row[, mixed field]) 3.0
    Gets result data

bool mysql_select_db(string database_name[, int link_identifier]) 3.0
    Selects a MySQL database

string mysql_stat([int link_identifier]) 4.3.0
    Returns a string containing status information

int mysql_thread_id([int link_identifier]) 4.3.0
    Returns the thread ID of current connection

resource mysql_unbuffered_query(string query[, int link_identifier][, int result_mode])   *4.0.6*
> Sends an SQL query to MySQL, without fetching and buffering the result rows

void natcasesort(array array_arg)   *4.0*
> Sorts an array using case-insensitive natural sort

void natsort(array array_arg)   *4.0*
> Sorts an array using natural sort

object new class_name()   *3.0*
> Language keyword that instantiates a class and returns the resulting object

mixed next(array array_arg)   *3.0*
> Moves array argument's internal pointer to the next element and returns it

string ngettext(string MSGID1, string MSGID2, int N)   *4.1.0*
> Plural version of gettext()

string nl2br(string str)   *3.0*
> Converts newlines to HTML line breaks

string nl_langinfo(int item)   *4.1.0*
> Queries language and locale information

string number_format(float number[, int num_decimal_places[, string dec_seperator, string thousands_seperator]])   *3.0*
> Formats a number with grouped thousands

bool ob_clean(void)   *4.1.0*
> Cleans (deletes) the current output buffer

bool ob_end_clean(void)   *4.0*
> Cleans the output buffer and then deletes current output buffer

bool ob_end_flush(void)   *4.0*
> Flushes (sends) the output buffer and then deletes current output buffer

bool ob_flush(void)   *4.1.0*
> Flushes (sends) contents of the output buffer

string ob_get_contents(void)   *4.0*
> Returns the contents of the output buffer

string ob_get_length(void)   *4.0.2*
    Returns the length of the output buffer

int ob_get_level(void)   *4.1.0*
    Returns the nesting level of the output buffer

false|array ob_get_status([bool full_status])   *4.1.0*
    Returns the status of the active or all output buffers

string ob_gzhandler(string str, int mode)   *4.0.4*
    Encodes str based on accept-encoding setting; designed to be
    called from ob_start()

string ob_iconv_handler(string contents, int status)   *4.0.5*
    Returns string in the output buffer converted into the
    iconv.output_encoding character set

void ob_implicit_flush([int flag])   *4.0*
    Turns implicit flush on/off; equivalent to calling flush() after
    every output call

false|array ob_list_handlers()   *4.3.0*
    Lists all output buffers in an array

bool ob_start([string|array user_function[, int chunk_size[, bool erase]]])   *4.0*
    Turns on output buffering (specifying an optional output
    handler)

int ocibindbyname(int stmt, string name, mixed &var,
int maxlength[, int type])   *3.0.4*
    Binds a PHP variable to an Oracle placeholder by name

int ocicancel(int stmt)   *3.0.8*
    Prepares a new row of data for reading

string ocicloselob(object lob)   *4.0.6*
    Closes a large object descriptor

string ocicollappend(object collection, object object)   *4.0.6*
    Appends an object to the collection

string ocicollassign(object collection,object object)   *4.0.6*
    Assigns a collection from another existing collection

string ocicollassignelem(object collection, string ndx, string val)   *4.0.6*
    Assigns element val to collection at index ndx

string ocicollgetelem(object collection, string ndx)   *4.0.6*
   Retrieves the value at collection index ndx

string ocicollmax(object collection)   *4.0.6*
   Returns the maximum value of a collection; for a varray this is
   the maximum length of the array

string ocicollsize(object collection)   *4.0.6*
   Returns the size of a collection

string ocicolltrim(object collection, int num)   *4.0.6*
   Trims num elements from the end of a collection

int ocicolumnisnull(int stmt, int col)   *3.0.4*
   Tells whether a column is NULL

string ocicolumnname(int stmt, int col)   *3.0.4*
   Tells the name of a column

int ocicolumnprecision(int stmt, int col)   *4.0*
   Tells the precision of a column

int ocicolumnscale(int stmt, int col)   *4.0*
   Tells the scale of a column

int ocicolumnsize(int stmt, int col)   *3.0.4*
   Tells the maximum data size of a column

mixed ocicolumntype(int stmt, int col)   *3.0.4*
   Tells the data type of a column

mixed ocicolumntyperaw(int stmt, int col)   *4.0*
   Tells the raw Oracle data type of a column

string ocicommit(int conn)   *3.0.7*
   Commits the current context

int ocidefinebyname(int stmt, string name, mixed &var[, int type])   *3.0.7*
   Defines a PHP variable to an Oracle column by name

array ocierror([int stmt|conn|global])   *3.0.7*
   Returns the last error of stmt|conn|global; returns false if no
   error has occurred

int ociexecute(int stmt[, int mode])   *3.0.4*
   Executes a parsed statement

int ocifetch(int stmt)   *3.0.4*
   Prepares a new row of data for reading

---

int ocifetchinto(int stmt, array &output[, int mode])   *3.0.4*
    Fetches a row of result data into an array

int ocifetchstatement(int stmt, array &output[, int skip][,
int maxrows][, int flags])   *3.0.8*
    Fetches all rows of result data into an array

string ocifreecollection(object lob)   *4.1.0*
    Deletes collection object

string ocifreedesc(object lob)   *4.0*
    Deletes large object description

int ocifreestatement(int stmt)   *3.0.5*
    Frees all resources associated with a statement

void ociinternaldebug(int onoff)   *3.0.4*
    Toggles internal debugging output for the OCI extension

string ociloadlob(object lob)   *4.0*
    Loads a large object

int ocilogoff(int conn)   *3.0.4*
    Disconnects from database

int ocilogon(string user, string pass[, string db])   *3.0.4*
    Connects to an Oracle database and logs on

string ocinewcollection(int connection, string tdo,[string schema])   *4.0.6*
    Initializes a new collection

int ocinewcursor(int conn)   *3.0.8*
    Returns a new cursor (statement handle); use to bind ref
    cursors

string ocinewdescriptor(int connection[, int type])   *3.0.7*
    Initializes a new empty LOB or FILE descriptor (LOB is
    default)

int ocinlogon(string user, string pass[, string db])   *3.0.8*
    Creates a new connection to an Oracle database and logs on;
    returns a new session

int ocinumcols(int stmt)   *3.0.4*
    Returns the number of result columns in a statement

int ociparse(int conn, string query)   *3.0.4*
    Parses a query and returns a statement

---

int ociplogon(string user, string pass[, string db])   *3.0.8*
> Connects to an Oracle database using a persistent connection and logs on

string ociresult(int stmt, mixed column)   *3.0.4*
> Returns a single column of result data

string ocirollback(int conn)   *3.0.7*
> Rolls back the current context

int ocirowcount(int stmt)   *3.0.7*
> Returns the row count of an OCI statement

string ocisavelob(object lob)   *4.0*
> Saves a large object

string ocisavelobfile(object lob)   *4.0*
> Saves a large object file

string ociserverversion(int conn)   *3.0.4*
> Returns a string containing server version information

int ocisetprefetch(int stmt, int prefetch_rows)   *3.0.12*
> Sets the number of rows to be prefetched for the statement

int ocistatementtype(int stmt)   *3.0.5*
> Returns the query type of an OCI statement

void ociwritelobtofile(object lob[, string filename][, int start][, int length])   *4.0*
> Writes a large object into a file

int ociwritetemporarylob(int stmt, int loc, string var)   *4.0.6*
> Returns the row count of an OCI statement

int octdec(string octal_number)   *3.0*
> Returns the decimal equivalent of an octal string

mixed opendir(string path)   *3.0*
> Opens a directory and returns a dir_handle

bool openlog(string ident, int option, int facility)   *3.0*
> Opens connection to system logger

OR   *4.0*
> Language keyword that is similar to the || operator, except lower precedence

int ord(string character)   *3.0*
> Returns ASCII value of character

void overload(string class_entry)   *4.1.0*
    Enables property and method call overloading for a class

string pack(string format, mixed arg1[, mixed arg2[, mixed ...]])   *3.0*
    Takes one or more arguments and packs them into a binary
    string according to the format argument

array parse_ini_file(string filename[, bool process_sections])   *4.0*
    Parses configuration file

void parse_str(string encoded_string[, array result])   *3.0*
    Parses GET/POST/Cookie data and sets global variables

array parse_url(string url)   *3.0*
    Parses a URL and returns its components

void passthru(string command[, int return_value])   *3.0*
    Executes an external program and displays raw output

array pathinfo(string path)   *4.0.3*
    Returns information about a certain string

int pclose(resource fp)   *3.0*
    Closes a file pointer opened by popen( )

int pcntl_alarm(int seconds)   *4.3.0*
    Sets an alarm clock for delivery of a signal

bool pcntl_exec(string path[, array args[, array envs]])   *4.1.0*
    Executes specified program in current process space as
    defined by exec( )

int pcntl_fork(void)   *4.1.0*
    Forks the currently running process following the same
    behavior as the Unix fork( ) system call

bool pcntl_signal(long signo, mixed handle)   *4.1.0*
    Assigns a system signal handler to a PHP function

int pcntl_waitpid(long pid, long status, long options)   *4.1.0*
    Waits on or returns the status of a forked child as defined by
    the waitpid( ) system call

int pcntl_wexitstatus(long status)   *4.1.0*
    Returns the status code of a child's exit

bool pcntl_wifexited(long status)   *4.1.0*
Returns true if the child status code represents a successful exit

bool pcntl_wifsignaled(long status)   *4.1.0*
Returns true if the child status code represents a process that was terminated due to a signal

bool pcntl_wifstopped(long status)   *4.1.0*
Returns true if the child status code represents a stopped process (WUNTRACED must have been used with waitpid())

int pcntl_wstopsig(long status)   *4.1.0*
Returns the number of the signal that caused the specified process to stop

int pcntl_wtermsig(long status)   *4.1.0*
Returns the number of the signal that terminated the specified process

void pdf_add_annotation(int pdfdoc, float xll, float yll, float xur, float xur, string title, string text)   *3.0.12*
Sets annotation (deprecated; use pdf_add_note() instead)

int pdf_add_bookmark(int pdfdoc, string text[, int parent, int open])   *4.0.1*
Adds bookmark for current page

void pdf_add_launchlink(int pdfdoc, float llx, float lly, float urx, float ury, string filename)   *4.0.5*
Adds link to web resource

void pdf_add_locallink(int pdfdoc, float llx, float lly, float urx, float ury, int page, string dest)   *4.0.5*
Adds link to web resource

void pdf_add_note(int pdfdoc, float llx, float lly, float urx, float ury, string contents, string title, string icon, int open)   *4.0.5*
Sets annotation

void pdf_add_pdflink(int pdfdoc, float llx, float lly, float urx, float ury, string filename, int page, string dest)   *3.0.12*
Adds link to PDF document

void pdf_add_thumbnail(int pdf, int image)   *4.0.5*
Adds an existing image as thumbnail for the current page.

void pdf_add_weblink(int pdfdoc, float llx, float lly, float urx, float ury, string url) *3.0.12*
    Adds link to web resource

void pdf_arc(int pdfdoc, float x, float y, float radius, float start, float end) *3.0.6*
    Draws an arc

void pdf_arcn(int pdf, float x, float y, float r, float alpha, float beta) *4.0.5*
    Draws a clockwise circular arc from alpha to beta degrees

void pdf_attach_file(int pdf, float lly, float lly, float urx, float ury, string filename, string description, string author, string mimetype, string icon) *4.0.5*
    Adds a file attachment annotation at the rectangle specified by the lower left and upper right corners

void pdf_begin_page(int pdfdoc, float width, float height) *3.0.6*
    Starts page

int pdf_begin_pattern(int pdf, float width, float height, float xstep, float ystep, int painttype) *4.0.5*
    Start a new pattern definition

int pdf_begin_template(int pdf, float width, float height) *4.0.5*
    Start a new template definition

void pdf_circle(int pdfdoc, float x, float y, float radius) *3.0.6*
    Draws a circle

void pdf_clip(int pdfdoc) *3.0.6*
    Clips to current path

void pdf_close(int pdfdoc) *3.0.6*
    Closes the PDF document

void pdf_close_image(int pdf, int pdfimage) *3.0.7*
    Closes the PDF image

void pdf_close_pdi(int pdf, int doc) *4.0.5*
    Closes all open page handles and closes the input PDF document

void pdf_close_pdi_page(int pdf, int page) *4.0.5*
    Closes the page handle and frees all page-related resources

void pdf_closepath(int pdfdoc) *3.0.6*
    Closes path

---

void pdf_closepath_fill_stroke(int pdfdoc) *3.0.6*
  Closes, fills, and strokes current path

void pdf_closepath_stroke(int pdfdoc) *3.0.6*
  Closes path and draws line along path

void pdf_concat(int pdf, float a, float b, float c, float d, float e, float f) *4.0.5*
  Concatenates a matrix to the current transformation matrix for text and graphics

void pdf_continue_text(int pdfdoc, string text) *3.0.6*
  Outputs text in next line

void pdf_curveto(int pdfdoc, float x1, float y1, float x2, float y2, float x3, float y3) *3.0.6*
  Draws a curve

bool pdf_delete(int pdfdoc) *4.0.5*
  Deletes the PDF object

void pdf_end_page(int pdfdoc) *3.0.6*
  Ends page

void pdf_end_pattern(int pdf) *4.0.5*
  Finishes the pattern definition

void pdf_end_template(int pdf) *4.0.5*
  Finishes the template definition

void pdf_endpath(int pdfdoc) *3.0.6*
  Ends current path

void pdf_fill(int pdfdoc) *3.0.6*
  Fills current path

void pdf_fill_stroke(int pdfdoc) *3.0.6*
  Fills and stroke current path

int pdf_findfont(int pdfdoc, string fontname, string encoding[, int embed]) *4.0.5*
  Prepares the font fontname for later use with pdf_setfont( )

int pdf_get_buffer(int pdfdoc) *4.0.5*
  Fetches the full buffer containing the generated PDF data

int pdf_get_font(int pdfdoc) *4.0*
  Gets the current font

---

string pdf_get_fontname(int pdfdoc) *4.0*
Gets the current font name

float pdf_get_fontsize(int pdfdoc) *4.0*
Gets the current font size

int pdf_get_image_height(int pdf, int pdfimage) *3.0.12*
Returns the height of an image

int pdf_get_image_width(int pdf, int pdfimage) *3.0.12*
Returns the width of an image

int pdf_get_majorversion() *4.1.0*
Returns the major version number of the PDFlib

int pdf_get_minorversion() *4.1.0*
Returns the minor version number of the PDFlib

string pdf_get_parameter(int pdfdoc, string key, mixed modifier) *4.0.1*
Gets arbitrary parameters

string pdf_get_pdi_parameter(int pdf, string key, int doc, int page, int index) *4.0.5*
Gets the contents of some PDI document parameter with string type

float pdf_get_pdi_value(int pdf, string key, int doc, int page, int index) *4.0.5*
Gets the contents of some PDI document parameter with numerical type

float pdf_get_value(int pdfdoc, string key, float modifier) *4.0.1*
Gets arbitrary value

void pdf_initgraphics(int pdf) *4.0.5*
Resets all implicit color and graphics state parameters to their defaults

void pdf_lineto(int pdfdoc, float x, float y) *3.0.6*
Draws a line

int pdf_makespotcolor(int pdf, string spotname) *4.0.5*
Makes a named spot color from the current color

void pdf_moveto(int pdfdoc, float x, float y) *3.0.6*
Sets current point

int pdf_new() *4.0.5*
Creates a new PDF object

---

int pdf_open([int filedesc])   *3.0.6*
> Opens a new PDF document (deprecated; use pdf_new() and pdf_open_file() instead)

int pdf_open_ccitt(int pdf, string filename, int width, int height,
int bitreverse, int k, int blackIs1)   *4.0.5*
> Opens an image file with raw CCITT G3 or G4 compressed bitmap data

int pdf_open_file(int pdfdoc[, char filename])   *4.0.5*
> Opens a new PDF document; if filename is NULL, document is created in memory

int pdf_open_gif(int pdf, string giffile)   *3.0.7*
> Opens a GIF file and returns an image for placement in a PDF document

int pdf_open_image(int pdf, string type, string source, string data,
long length, int width, int height, int components, int bpc, string params)   *4.0.5*
> Opens an image of the given type and returns an image for placement in a PDF document

int pdf_open_image_file(int pdf, string type, string file,
string stringparam, int intparam)   *3 CVS Only*
> Opens an image file of the given type and returns an image for placement in a PDF document

int pdf_open_jpeg(int pdf, string jpegfile)   *3.0.7*
> Opens a JPEG file and returns an image for placement in a PDF document

int pdf_open_memory_image(int pdf, int image)   *3.0.10*
> Takes an GD image and returns an image for placement in a PDF document

int pdf_open_pdi(int pdf, string filename, string stringparam,
int intparam)   *4.0.5*
> Opens an existing PDF document and prepare it for later use

int pdf_open_pdi_page(int pdf, int doc, int page, string label)   *4.0.5*
> Prepares a page for later use with pdf_place_image()

int pdf_open_png(int pdf, string pngfile)   *4.0*
> Opens a PNG file and returns an image for placement in a PDF document

int pdf_open_tiff(int pdf, string tifffile)   *4.0*

> Opens a TIFF file and returns an image for placement in a PDF document

void pdf_place_image(int pdf, int pdfimage, float x, float y, float scale)   *3.0.7*

> Places image in the PDF document

void pdf_place_pdi_page(int pdf, int page, float x, float y, float sx, float sy) *4.0.6*

> Places a PDF page with lower left corner at x, y and scales it

void pdf_rect(int pdfdoc, float x, float y, float width, float height)   *3.0.6*

> Draws a rectangle

void pdf_restore(int pdfdoc)   *3.0.6*

> Restores formerly saved environment

void pdf_rotate(int pdfdoc, float angle)   *3.0.6*

> Sets rotation

void pdf_save(int pdfdoc)   *3.0.6*

> Saves current environment

void pdf_scale(int pdfdoc, float x_scale, float y_scale)   *3.0.6*

> Sets scaling

void pdf_set_border_color(int pdfdoc, float red, float green, float blue)   *3.0.12*

> Sets color of box surrounding annotations and links

void pdf_set_border_dash(int pdfdoc, float black, float white)   *4.0.1*

> Sets the border dash style of annotations and links

void pdf_set_border_style(int pdfdoc, string style, float width) *3.0.12*

> Sets style of box surrounding annotations and links

void pdf_set_char_spacing(int pdfdoc, float space)   *3.0.6*

> Sets character spacing

void pdf_set_duration(int pdfdoc, float duration)   *3.0.6*

> Sets duration between pages

void pdf_set_font(int pdfdoc, string font, float size,
string encoding[, int embed])   *3.0.6*

> Selects the current font face, size, and encoding

void pdf_set_horiz_scaling(int pdfdoc, float scale)   *3.0.6*

> Sets horizontal scaling of text

bool pdf_set_info(int pdfdoc, string fieldname, string value)   *4.0.1*

> Fills an information field of the document

---

bool pdf_set_info_author(int pdfdoc, string author)   *3.0.6*
    Fills the author field of the document

bool pdf_set_info_creator(int pdfdoc, string creator)   *3.0.6*
    Fills the creator field of the document

bool pdf_set_info_keywords(int pdfdoc, string keywords)   *3.0.6*
    Fills the keywords field of the document

bool pdf_set_info_subject(int pdfdoc, string subject)   *3.0.6*
    Fills the subject field of the document

bool pdf_set_info_title(int pdfdoc, string title)   *3.0.6*
    Fills the title field of the document

void pdf_set_leading(int pdfdoc, float distance)   *3.0.6*
    Sets distance between text lines

void pdf_set_parameter(int pdfdoc, string key, string value)   *4.0*
    Sets arbitrary parameters

void pdf_set_text_pos(int pdfdoc, float x, float y)   *3.0.6*
    Sets the position of text for the next pdf_show() call

void pdf_set_text_rendering(int pdfdoc, int mode)   *3.0.6*
    Determines how text is rendered

void pdf_set_text_rise(int pdfdoc, float value)   *3.0.6*
    Sets the text rise

void pdf_set_transition(int pdfdoc, int transition)   *3.0.6*
    Sets transitions between pages

void pdf_set_value(int pdfdoc, string key, float value)   *4.0.1*
    Sets arbitrary value

void pdf_set_word_spacing(int pdfdoc, float space)   *3.0.6*
    Sets spacing between words

**void pdf_setcolor(int pdf, string type, string colorspace,
float c1[, float c2[, float c3[, float c4]]])**   *4.0.5*
    Sets the current color space and color.

void pdf_setdash(int pdfdoc, float black, float white)   *3.0.6*
    Sets dash pattern

void pdf_setflat(int pdfdoc, float value)   *3.0.6*
    Sets flatness

void pdf_setfont(int pdfdoc, int font, float fontsize)   4.0.5
  Sets the current font in the given fontsize

void pdf_setgray(int pdfdoc, float value)   3.0.6
  Sets drawing and filling color to gray value

void pdf_setgray_fill(int pdfdoc, float value)   3.0.6
  Sets filling color to gray value

void pdf_setgray_stroke(int pdfdoc, float value)   3.0.6
  Sets drawing color to gray value

void pdf_setlinecap(int pdfdoc, int value)   3.0.6
  Sets line cap parameter

void pdf_setlinejoin(int pdfdoc, int value)   3.0.6
  Sets line join parameter

void pdf_setlinewidth(int pdfdoc, float width)   3.0.6
  Sets line width

void pdf_setmatrix(int pdf, float a, float b, float c, float d, float e, float f)   4.0.5
  Sets the current transformation matrix

void pdf_setmiterlimit(int pdfdoc, float value)   3.0.6
  Sets miter limit

void pdf_setpolydash(int pdfdoc, float darray)   4.0.5
  Sets more complicated dash pattern

void pdf_setrgbcolor(int pdfdoc, float red, float green, float blue) 3.0.6
  Sets drawing and filling color to RGB color value

void pdf_setrgbcolor_fill(int pdfdoc, float red, float green, float blue)   3.0.6
  Sets filling color to RGB color value

void pdf_setrgbcolor_stroke(int pdfdoc, float red, float green, float blue) 3.0.6
  Sets drawing color to RGB color value

void pdf_show(int pdfdoc, string text)   3.0.6
  Outputs text at current position

**int pdf_show_boxed(int pdfdoc, string text, float x_koor,
float y_koor, float width, float height, string mode[, string feature])**   4.0
  Outputs text formatted in a boxed

void pdf_show_xy(int pdfdoc, string text, float x_koor, float y_koor)   3.0.6
  Outputs text at position

---

void pdf_skew(int pdfdoc, float xangle, float yangle)   4.0
  Skews the coordinate system

float pdf_stringwidth(int pdfdoc, string text[, int font, float size])   3.0.6
  Returns width of text in current font

void pdf_stroke(int pdfdoc)   3.0.6
  Draws line along path

void pdf_translate(int pdfdoc, float x, float y)   3.0.6
  Sets origin of coordinate system

int pfsockopen(string hostname, int port[, int errno[,
string errstr[, float timeout]]])   3.0.7
  Opens persistent Internet or Unix domain socket connection

int pg_affected_rows(resource result)   4.1.0
  Returns the number of affected tuples

bool pg_cancel_query(resource connection)   4.1.0
  Cancels request

string pg_client_encoding([resource connection])   3 CVS Only
  Gets the current client encoding

bool pg_close([resource connection])   3.0
  Closes a PostgreSQL connection

resource pg_connect([[string connection_string] | [string host,
string port[, string options[, string tty,]] string database)   3.0
  Opens a PostgreSQL connection

bool pg_connection_busy(resource connection)   4.1.0
  Gets whether connection is busy or not

bool pg_connection_reset(resource connection)   4.1.0
  Resets connection (reconnects)

int pg_connection_status(resource connnection)   4.1.0
  Gets connection status

array pg_convert(resource db, string table, array values[, int options])   4.3.0
  Checks and converts values for PostgreSQL SQL statement

bool pg_copy_from(int connection, string table_name,
array rows[, string delimiter[, string null_as]])   4.1.0
  Copies table from array

**array pg_copy_to(int connection, string table_name[,
string delimiter[, string null_as]])**   *4.1.0*
    Copies table to array

string pg_dbname([resource connection])   *3.0*
    Gets the database name

bool pg_delete(resource db, string table, array ids[, int options])   *4.3.0*
    Deletes records with values in ids

bool pg_end_copy([resource connection])   *4.0.3*
    Completes the a copy command by syncing with the backend

string pg_escape_bytea(string data)   *4.1.0*
    Escapes a string for the bytea type

string pg_escape_string(string data)   *4.1.0*
    Escapes a string for text/char type

array pg_fetch_all(resource result)   *4.3.0*
    Fetches all rows into array

array pg_fetch_array(resource result[, int row[, int result_type]])   *3.0.1*
    Fetches a row as an array

object pg_fetch_object(resource result[, int row[, int result_type]])   *3.0.1*
    Fetches a row as an object

**mixed pg_fetch_result(resource result, [int row_number,]
mixed field_name)**   *4.1.0*
    Returns values from a result identifier

array pg_fetch_row(resource result[, int row[, int result_type]])   *3.0.1*
    Gets a row as an enumerated array

**int pg_field_is_null(resource result, [int row,]
mixed field_name_or_number)**   *4.1.0*
    Tests if a field is NULL

string pg_field_name(resource result, int field_number)   *4.1.0*
    Returns the name of the field

int pg_field_num(resource result, string field_name)   *4.1.0*
    Returns the field number of the named field

**int pg_field_prtlen(resource result, [int row,]
mixed field_name_or_number)**   *4.1.0*
    Returns the printed length

---

int pg_field_size(resource result, int field_number) *4.1.0*
    Returns the internal size of the field

string pg_field_type(resource result, int field_number) *4.1.0*
    Returns the type name for the given field

bool pg_free_result(resource result) *4.1.0*
    Frees result memory

resource pg_get_result([resource connection]) *4.1.0*
    Gets asynchronous query result

string pg_host([resource connection]) *3.0*
    Returns the hostname associated with the connection

bool pg_insert(resource db, string table, array values[, int options]) *4.3.0*
    Inserts an array of values into table

string pg_last_error([resource connection]) *4.1.0*
    Gets the error message string

string pg_last_notice(resource connection) *4.0.6*
    Returns the last notice set by the backend

string pg_last_oid(resource result) *4.1.0*
    Returns the last object identifier

bool pg_lo_close(resource large_object) *4.1.0*
    Closes a large object

int pg_lo_create([resource connection]) *4.1.0*
    Creates a large object

bool pg_lo_export([resource connection,] int objoid, string filename) *4.1.0*
    Exports a large object directly to filesystem

int pg_lo_import([resource connection,] string filename) *4.1.0*
    Imports a large object directly from filesystem

resource pg_lo_open([resource connection,] int large_object_oid, string mode) *4.1.0*
    Opens a large object and returns the file descriptor

string pg_lo_read(resource large_object[, int len]) *4.1.0*
    Reads a large object

int pg_lo_read_all(resource large_object) *4.1.0*
    Reads a large object and sends it straight to the browser

bool pg_lo_seek(resource large_object, int offset[, int whence])   *4.1.0*
    Seeks position of large object

int pg_lo_tell(resource large_object)   *4.1.0*
    Returns current position of large object

bool pg_lo_unlink([resource connection,] string large_object_oid)   *4.1.0*
    Deletes a large object

int pg_lo_write(resource large_object, string buf[, int len])   *4.1.0*
    Writes a large object

array pg_metadata(resource db, string table)   *4.3.0*
    Gets metadata

int pg_num_fields(resource result)   *4.1.0*
    Returns the number of fields in the result

int pg_num_rows(resource result)   *4.1.0*
    Returns the number of rows in the result

string pg_options([resource connection])   *3.0*
    Gets the options associated with the connection

resource pg_pconnect([string connection_string] | [string host,
string port[, string options[, string tty,]] string database)   *3.0*
    Opens a persistent PostgreSQL connection

int pg_port([resource connection])   *3.0*
    Returns the port number associated with the connection

bool pg_put_line([resource connection,] string query)   *4.0.3*
    Sends null-terminated string to backend server

resource pg_query([resource connection,] string query)   *4.1.0*
    Executes a query

string pg_result_error(resource result)   *4.1.0*
    Gets error message associated with result

int pg_result_status(resource result[, long result_type])   *4.1.0*
    Gets status of query result

array pg_select(resource db, string table, array ids[, int options])   *4.3.0*
    Selects records that have values in ids

bool pg_send_query(resource connection, string qeury)   *4.1.0*
    Sends asynchronous query

int pg_set_client_encoding([resource connection,]
string encoding)   *3 CVS Only*
    Sets client encoding

bool pg_trace(string filename[, string mode[, resource connection]])   *4.0.1*
    Enables tracing a PostgreSQL connection

string pg_tty([resource connection])   *3.0*
    Returns the tty name associated with the connection

bool pg_untrace([resource connection])   *4.0.1*
    Disables tracing of a PostgreSQL connection

bool pg_update(resource db, string table, array fields,
array ids[, int options])   *4.3.0*
    Updates table using values in fields and ids

string php_sapi_name(void)   *4.0.1*
    Returns the current SAPI module name

string php_uname(void)   *4.0.2*
    Returns information about the system PHP was built on

void phpcredits([int flag])   *4.0*
    Prints the list of people who have contributed to the PHP
    project

void phpinfo([int what])   *3.0*
    Outputs a page of useful information about PHP and the
    current request

string phpversion([string extension])   *3.0*
    Returns the current PHP version

float pi(void)   *3.0*
    Returns an approximation of pi

void png2wbmp (string f_org, string f_dest, int d_height,
int d_width, int threshold)   *4.0.5*
    Converts PNG image to WBMP image

resource popen(string command, string mode)   *3.0*
    Executes a command and opens either a read or a write pipe
    to it

string posix_ctermid(void)   *3.0.13*
    Generates terminal path name (POSIX.1, 4.7.1)

int posix_get_last_error(void)   *4.1.0*

Retrieves the error number set by the last Posix function that failed.

string posix_getcwd(void)   *3.0.13*

Gets working directory pathname (POSIX.1, 5.2.2)

int posix_getegid(void)   *3.0.10*

Gets the current effective group ID (POSIX.1, 4.2.1)

int posix_geteuid(void)   *3.0.10*

Gets the current effective user ID (POSIX.1, 4.2.1)

int posix_getgid(void)   *3.0.10*

Gets the current group ID (POSIX.1, 4.2.1)

array posix_getgrgid(long gid)   *3.0.13*

Gets information about a group by group ID (POSIX.1, 9.2.1)

array posix_getgrnam(string groupname)   *3.0.13*

Gets information about a group by group name (POSIX.1, 9.2.1)

array posix_getgroups(void)   *3.0.10*

Gets supplementary group IDs (POSIX.1, 4.2.3)

string posix_getlogin(void)   *3.0.13*

Gets user name (POSIX.1, 4.2.4)

int posix_getpgid(void)   *3.0.10*

Gets the process group ID of the specified process (not a POSIX function, but a SVR4ism, so we compile conditionally)

int posix_getpgrp(void)   *3.0.10*

Gets current process group ID (POSIX.1, 4.3.1)

int posix_getpid(void)   *3.0.10*

Gets the current process ID (POSIX.1, 4.1.1)

int posix_getppid(void)   *3.0.10*

Gets the parent process ID (POSIX.1, 4.1.1)

array posix_getpwnam(string groupname)   *3.0.13*

Gets information about a user by username (POSIX.1, 9.2.2)

array posix_getpwuid(long uid)   *3.0.13*

Gets information about a user by user ID (POSIX.1, 9.2.2)

int posix_getrlimit(void)   *3.0.10*

    Gets system resource consumption limits (not a POSIX function, but a BSDism and a SVR4ism, so we compile conditionally)

int posix_getsid(void)   *3.0.10*

    Gets process group ID of session leader (not a POSIX function, but a SVR4ism, so we compile conditionally)

int posix_getuid(void)   *3.0.10*

    Gets the current user ID (POSIX.1, 4.2.1)

bool posix_isatty(int fd)   *3.0.13*

    Determine if file descriptor is a tty (POSIX.1, 4.7.1)

bool posix_kill(int pid, int sig)   *3.0.13*

    Sends a signal to a process (POSIX.1, 3.3.2)

bool posix_mkfifo(string pathname, int mode)   *3.0.13*

    Makes a FIFO special file (POSIX.1, 5.4.2)

bool posix_setegid(long uid)   *4.0.2*

    Sets effective group ID

bool posix_seteuid(long uid)   *4.0.2*

    Sets effective user ID

bool posix_setgid(int uid)   *3.0.13*

    Sets group ID (POSIX.1, 4.2.2)

bool posix_setpgid(int pid, int pgid)   *3.0.13*

    Sets process group ID for job control (POSIX.1, 4.3.3)

int posix_setsid(void)   *3.0.13*

    Creates session and sets process group ID (POSIX.1, 4.3.2)

bool posix_setuid(long uid)   *3.0.13*

    Sets user ID (POSIX.1, 4.2.2)

string posix_strerror(int errno)   *4.1.0*

    Retrieves the system error message associated with the given errno

array posix_times(void)   *3.0.13*

    Gets process times (POSIX.1, 4.5.2)

string posix_ttyname(int fd)   *3.0.13*

    Determines terminal device name (POSIX.1, 4.7.2)

array posix_uname(void) *3.0.10*
    Gets system name (POSIX.1, 4.4.1)

number pow(number base, number exponent) *3.0*
    Returns base raised to the power of exponent (as an integer result when possible)

array preg_grep(string regex, array input) *4.0*
    Searches array and returns entries that match regex

int preg_match(string pattern, string subject[, array subpatterns[, int flags]]) *3.0.9*
    Performs a Perl-style regular expression match

int preg_match_all(string pattern, string subject, array subpatterns[, int flags]) *3.0.9*
    Performs a Perl-style global regular expression match

string preg_quote(string str, string delim_char) *3.0.9*
    Quotes regular expression characters plus an optional character

string preg_replace(mixed regex, mixed replace, mixed subject[, int limit]) *3.0.9*
    Performs Perl-style regular expression replacement.

string preg_replace_callback(mixed regex, mixed callback, mixed subject[, int limit]) *4.0.5*
    Performs Perl-style regular expression replacement using replacement callback.

array preg_split(string pattern, string subject[, int limit[, int flags]]) *3.0.9*
    Splits string into an array using a Perl-style regular expression as a delimiter

mixed prev(array array_arg) *3.0*
    Moves an array's internal pointer to the previous element and returns it

bool print(string arg) *3.0*
    Outputs a string

bool print_r(mixed var[, bool return]) *4.0*
    Prints out or returns information about the specified variable

int printf(string format[, mixed arg1[, mixed ...]]) *3.0*
    Outputs a formatted string

int proc_close(resource process)   *4.3.0*
    Closes a process opened by proc_open()

resource proc_open(string command, array descriptorspec, array &pipes)   *4.3.0*
    Run a process with more control over its file descriptors

int pspell_add_to_personal(int pspell, string word)   *4.0.2*
    Adds a word to a personal list

int pspell_add_to_session(int pspell, string word)   *4.0.2*
    Adds a word to the current session

int pspell_check(int pspell, string word)   *4.0.2*
    Returns true if word is valid

int pspell_clear_session(int pspell)   *4.0.2*
    Clears the current session

int pspell_config_create(string language[, string spelling[,
string jargon[, string encoding]]])   *4.0.2*
    Creates a new configuration to be used later to create a manager

int pspell_config_ignore(int conf, int ignore)   *4.0.2*
    Ignore words with ignore characters or less

int pspell_config_mode(int conf, long mode)   *4.0.2*
    Selects mode for configuration (PSPELL_FAST, PSPELL_NORMAL, or PSPELL_BAD_SPELLERS)

int pspell_config_personal(int conf, string personal)   *4.0.2*
    Uses a personal dictionary for this configuration

int pspell_config_repl(int conf, string repl)   *4.0.2*
    Uses a personal dictionary with replacement pairs for this configuration

int pspell_config_runtogether(int conf, bool runtogether)   *4.0.2*
    Considers run-together words as valid components

int pspell_config_save_repl(int conf, bool save)   *4.0.2*
    Saves replacement pairs when a personal list is saved for this configuration

int pspell_new(string language[, string spelling[, string jargon[,
string encoding[, int mode]]]])   *4.0.2*
    Loads a dictionary

int pspell_new_config(int config) *4.0.2*
    Loads a dictionary based on the given configuration

int pspell_new_personal(string personal, string language[,
string spelling[, string jargon[, string encoding[, int mode]]]]) *4.0.2*
    Loads a dictionary with a personal word list

int pspell_save_wordlist(int pspell) *4.0.2*
    Saves the current (personal) wordlest

int pspell_store_replacement(int pspell, string misspell, string correct) *4.0.2*
    Notifies the dictionary of a user-selected replacement

array pspell_suggest(int pspell, string word) *4.0.2*
    Returns array of suggestions

bool putenv(string setting) *3.0*
    Sets the value of an environment variable

string quoted_printable_decode(string str) *3.0.6*
    Converts a quoted-printable string to an 8 bit string

string quotemeta(string str) *3.0*
    Quotes meta characters

float rad2deg(float number) *3.0.4*
    Converts the radian number to the equivalent number in degrees

int rand([int min, int max]) *3.0*
    Returns a random number

array range(mixed low, mixed high) *3.0.8*
    Creates an array containing the range of integers or characters from low to high (inclusive)

string rawurldecode(string str) *3.0*
    Decodes a URL-encoded string

string rawurlencode(string str) *3.0*
    URL-encodes a string

string readdir([resource dir_handle]) *3.0*
    Reads directory entry from `dir_handle`

int readfile(string filename[, int use_include_path]) *3.0*
    Outputs a file or a URL

int readgzfile(string filename[, int use_include_path])   *3.0*
    Outputs a .gz file

string readlink(string filename)   *3.0*
    Returns the target of a symbolic link

string realpath(string path)   *4.0*
    Returns the resolved path

bool recode_file(string request, resource input, resource output)   *3.0.13*
    Recodes file input into file output according to request

string recode_string(string request, string str)   *3.0.13*
    Recodes string str according to request string

void register_shutdown_function(string function_name)   *3.0.4*
    Registers a user-level function to be called on request termination

bool register_tick_function(string function_name[, mixed arg[, mixed ...]]) *4.0.3*
    Registers a tick callback function

bool rename(string old_name, string new_name)   *3.0*
    Renames a file

bool require filename   *3.0*
    Includes and evaluates the given file, with a fatal error on failure

bool require_once filename   *4.0*
    Includes and evaluates the given file if not already included, with a fatal error on failure

mixed reset(array array_arg)   *3.0*
    Sets an array's internal pointer to the first element and returns it

void restore_error_handler(void)   *4.0.1*
    Restores the previously defined error handler function

return(mixed result)   *3.0*
    Language keyword that returns its argument from a function or from current execution scope

bool rewind(resource fp)   *3.0*
    Rewinds the position of a file pointer

void rewinddir([resource dir_handle])   *3.0*
    Rewinds dir_handle back to the start

---

bool rmdir(string dirname)   *3.0*
> Removes a directory

float round(float number[, int precision])   *3.0*
> Returns the number rounded to specified precision

bool rsort(array array_arg[, int sort_flags])   *3.0*
> Sorts an array in reverse order

string rtrim(string str[, string character_mask])   *3.0*
> Removes trailing whitespace

int sem_acquire(int id)   *3.0.6*
> Acquires the semaphore with the given ID, blocking if necessary

int sem_get(int key[, int max_acquire[, int perm[, int auto_release]]])   *3.0.6*
> Returns an ID for the semaphore with the given key and allows max_acquire (default 1) processes to acquire it simultaneously

int sem_release(int id)   *3.0.6*
> Releases the semaphore with the given ID

int sem_remove(int id)   *4.1.0*
> Removes semaphore from Unix systems

string serialize(mixed variable)   *3.0.5*
> Returns a string representation of variable (that can later be unserialized)

int session_cache_expire([int new_cache_expire])   *4.1.0*
> Returns the current cache_expire; if new_cache_expire is given, the current cache_expire is replaced with new_cache_expire

string session_cache_limiter([string new_cache_limiter])   *4.0.3*
> Returns the current cache_limiter; if new_cache_limiter is given, the current cache_limiter is replaced with new_cache_limiter

bool session_decode(string data)   *4.0*
> Deserializes data and reinitializes the variables

bool session_destroy(void)   *4.0*
> Destroys the current session and all data associated with it

---

string session_encode(void)   *4.0*

Serializes the current setup and returns the serialized representation

array session_get_cookie_params(void)   *4.0*

Returns the session cookie parameters

string session_id([string newid])   *4.0*

Returns the current session ID; if newid is given, the session ID is replaced with newid

bool session_is_registered(string varname)   *4.0*

Checks if a variable is registered in the session

string session_module_name([string newname])   *4.0*

Returns the current module name used for accessing session data; if newname is given, the module name is replaced with newname

string session_name([string newname])   *4.0*

Returns the current session name; if newname is given, the session name is replaced with newname

bool session_register(mixed var_names[, mixed ...])   *4.0*

Adds variable name(s) to the list of variables that are frozen at the session end

string session_save_path([string newname])   *4.0*

Returns the current save path; if newname is given, the save path is replaced with newname

void session_set_cookie_params(int lifetime[, string path[, string domain[, bool secure]]])   *4.0*

Sets session cookie parameters

void session_set_save_handler(string open, string close, string read, string write, string destroy, string gc)   *4.0*

Sets user-level functions

bool session_start(void)   *4.0*

Begins a session by reinitializing frozen variables, registers browsers, etc.

bool session_unregister(string varname)   *4.0*

Removes varname from the list of variables that are frozen at the session end

---

void session_unset(void)   *4.0*
    Unsets all registered variables

void session_write_close(void)   *4.0.4*
    Writes session data and ends session

string set_error_handler(string error_handler)   *4.0.1*
    Sets a user-defined error handler function; returns the previously defined error handler, or false on error

int set_file_buffer(resource fp, int buffer)   *3.0.8*
    Sets file write buffer

bool set_magic_quotes_runtime(int new_setting)   *3.0.6*
    Sets the current active configuration setting of magic_quotes_runtime and returns previous setting

bool set_socket_blocking(resource socket, int mode)   *3.0*
    Sets blocking/non-blocking mode on a socket

bool set_time_limit(int seconds)   *3.0*
    Sets the maximum time a script can run

bool setcookie(string name[, string value[, int expires[, string path[, string domain[, bool secure]]]]])   *3.0*
    Sends a cookie

string setlocale(mixed category, string locale)   *3.0*
    Sets locale information

bool settype(mixed var, string type)   *3.0*
    Sets the type of the variable

string sha1(string str)   *4.3.0*
    Calculates the sha1 hash of a string

string sha1_file(string filename)   *4.3.0*
    Calculates the sha1 hash of given filename

string shell_exec(string cmd)   *4.0*
    Executes command via shell and returns complete output as string

int shm_attach(int key[, int memsize[, int perm]])   *3.0.6*
    Creates or opens a shared memory segment

int shm_detach(int shm_identifier)   *3.0.6*
    Disconnects from shared memory segment

---

mixed shm_get_var(int id, int variable_key)   *3.0.6*
   Returns a variable from shared memory

int shm_put_var(int shm_identifier, int variable_key, mixed variable)   *3.0.6*
   Inserts or updates a variable in shared memory

int shm_remove(int shm_identifier)   *3.0.6*
   Removes shared memory from Unix systems

int shm_remove_var(int id, int variable_key)   *3.0.6*
   Removes variable from shared memory

void shmop_close (int shmid)   *4.0.4*
   Closes a shared memory segment

bool shmop_delete (int shmid)   *4.0.4*
   Marks segment for deletion

int shmop_open (int key, int flags, int mode, int size)   *4.0.4*
   Gets and attaches a shared memory segment

string shmop_read (int shmid, int start, int count)   *4.0.4*
   Reads from a shared memory segment

int shmop_size (int shmid)   *4.0.4*
   Returns the shared memory size

int shmop_write (int shmid, string data, int offset)   *4.0.4*
   Writes to a shared memory segment

bool shuffle(array array_arg)   *3.0.8*
   Randomly shuffles the contents of an array

int similar_text(string str1, string str2[, float percent])   *3.0.7*
   Calculates the similarity between two strings

float sin(float number)   *3.0*
   Returns the sine of the number in radians

float sinh(float number)   *4.1.0*
   Returns the hyperbolic sine of the number

void sleep(int seconds)   *3.0*
   Delays for a given number of seconds

bool snmp_get_quick_print(void)   *3.0.8*
   Returns the current status of `quick_print`

void snmp_set_quick_print(int quick_print)   *3.0.8*
    Sets the value of `quick_print`

string snmpget(string host, string community, string object_id[,
int timeout[, int retries]])   *3.0*
    Fetches a SNMP object

array snmprealwalk(string host, string community, string object_id[,
int timeout[, int retries]])   *3.0.8*
    Returns all objects, including their respective object IDs, within the specified one

int snmpset(string host, string community, string object_id, string type,
mixed value[, int timeout[, int retries]])   *3.0.12*
    Sets the value of a SNMP object

array snmpwalk(string host, string community, string object_id[,
int timeout[, int retries]])   *3.0*
    Returns all objects under the specified object ID

resource socket_accept(resource socket)   *4.1.0*
    Accepts a connection on the listening socket

bool socket_bind(resource socket, string addr[, int port])   *4.1.0*
    Binds an open socket to a listening port; port is only specified in AF_INET family

void socket_clear_error([resource socket])   *4.1.0*
    Clears the error on the socket or the last error code

void socket_close(resource socket)   *4.1.0*
    Closes a file descriptor

bool socket_connect(resource socket, string addr[, int port])   *4.1.0*
    Opens a connection to `addr:port` on the socket specified by socket

resource socket_create(int domain, int type, int protocol)   *4.1.0*
    Creates an endpoint for communication in the domain specified by domain, of type specified by type

resource socket_create_listen(int port[, int backlog])   *4.1.0*
    Opens a socket on port to accept connections

bool socket_create_pair(int domain, int type, int protocol, array &fd) *4.1.0*
    Creates a pair of indistinguishable sockets and stores them in fd

---

mixed socket_get_option(resource socket, int level, int optname)   *4.3.0*
  Gets socket options for the socket

array socket_get_status(resource socket_descriptor)   *4.0*
  Returns an array describing socket status

bool socket_getpeername(resource socket, string &addr[, int &port])   *4.1.0*
  Queries the remote side of the given socket, which may result
  in either a host/port or a Unix filesystem path, depending on
  its type

bool socket_getsockname(resource socket, string &addr[, int &port])   *4.1.0*
  Queries the remote side of the given socket, which may result
  in either a host/port or a Unix filesystem path, depending on
  its type

bool socket_iovec_add(resource iovec, int iov_len)   *4.1.0*
  Adds a new vector to the scatter/gather array

resource socket_iovec_alloc(int num_vectors[, int ...])   *4.1.0*
  Builds a struct iovec for use with sendmsg(), recvmsg(),
  writev(), and readv()

bool socket_iovec_delete(resource iovec, int iov_pos)   *4.1.0*
  Deletes a vector from an array of vectors

string socket_iovec_fetch(resource iovec, int iovec_position)   *4.1.0*
  Returns the data that is stored in the iovec specified by
  iovec_id[iovec_position]

bool socket_iovec_free(resource iovec)   *4.1.0*
  Frees the iovec specified by iovec_id

bool socket_iovec_set(resource iovec, int iovec_position, string new_val)   *4.1.0*
  Sets the data held in iovec_id[iovec_position] to new_val

int socket_last_error([resource socket])   *4.1.0*
  Returns the last socket error (either the last used or the
  provided socket resource)

bool socket_listen(resource socket[, int backlog])   *4.1.0*
  Listens for a connection on a socket; backlog sets the
  maximum number of connections allowed to be waiting

string socket_read(resource socket, int length[, int type])   *4.1.0*
  Reads a maximum of length bytes from socket

bool socket_readv(resource socket, resource iovec_id)   *4.1.0*
    Reads from an file descriptor, using the scatter-gather array defined by iovec_id

int socket_recv(resource socket, string &buf, int len, int flags)   *4.1.0*
    Receives data from a connected socket

int socket_recvfrom(resource socket, string &buf, int len, int flags, string &name[, int &port])   *4.1.0*
    Receives data from a socket, connected or not

bool socket_recvmsg(resource socket, resource iovec, array &control, int &controllen, int &flags, string &addr[, int &port])   *4.1.0*
    Receives messages on a socket, whether connection-oriented or not

int socket_select(array &read_fds, array &write_fds, &array except_fds, int tv_sec[, int tv_usec])   *4.1.0*
    Runs the select() system call on the arrays of sockets with timeouts specified by tv_sec and tv_usec

int socket_send(resource socket, string buf, int len, int flags)   *4.1.0*
    Sends data to a connected socket

bool socket_sendmsg(resource socket, resource iovec, int flags, string addr[, int port])   *4.1.0*
    Sends a message to a socket, regardless of whether it is connection-oriented or not

int socket_sendto(resource socket, string buf, int len, int flags, string addr[, int port])   *4.1.0*
    Sends a message to a socket, whether it is connected or not

bool socket_set_block(resource socket)   *4.1.0*
    Sets blocking mode on a socket resource

bool socket_set_blocking(resource socket, int mode)   *4.0*
    Set blocking/non-blocking mode on a socket

bool socket_set_nonblock(resource socket)   *4.1.0*
    Sets non-blocking mode on a socket resource

bool socket_set_option(resource socket, int level, int optname, int|array optval)   *4.3.0*
    Sets socket options for the socket

bool socket_set_timeout(int socket_descriptor, int seconds,
int microseconds)   *4.0*
    Sets timeout on a socket read to seconds plus microseonds

bool socket_shutdown(resource socket[, int how])   *4.1.0*
    Shuts down a socket for receiving, sending, or both

string socket_strerror(int errno)   *4.1.0*
    Returns a string describing an error

int socket_write(resource socket, string buf[, int length])   *4.1.0*
    Writes the buffer to the socket resource

bool socket_writev(resource socket, resource iovec_id)   *4.1.0*
    Writes to a file descriptor using the scatter-gather array
    defined by iovec_id

bool sort(array array_arg[, int sort_flags])   *3.0*
    Sorts an array

string soundex(string str)   *3.0*
    Calculates the soundex key of a string

array split(string pattern, string string[, int limit])   *3.0*
    Splits a string into an array with a regular expression

array spliti(string pattern, string string[, int limit])   *4.0.1*
    Splits a string into an array with a case-insensitive regular
    expression

string sprintf(string format[, mixed arg1[, mixed ...]])   *3.0*
    Returns a formatted string

string sql_regcase(string string)   *3.0*
    Makes a regular expression for a case-insensitive match

float sqrt(float number)   *3.0*
    Returns the square root of the number

void srand([int seed])   *3.0*
    Seeds random number generator

mixed sscanf(string str, string format[, string ...])   *4.0.1*
    Implements an ANSI C compatible sscanf()

array stat(string filename)   *3.0*
    Gives information about a file

static var1[,var2[, ...]] *3.0*

Language keyword used inside functions in order to mark a variable as static

string str_pad(string input, int pad_length[, string pad_string[, int pad_type]]) *4.0.1*

Returns input string padded on the left or right to specified length with `pad_string`

string str_repeat(string input, int mult) *4.0*

Returns the input string repeated `mult` times

mixed str_replace(mixed search, mixed replace, mixed subject[, bool boyer]) *3.0.6*

Replaces all occurrences of search in subject with replace

string str_rot13(string str) *4.1.0*

Performs the rot13 transform on a string

int strcasecmp(string str1, string str2) *3.0.2*

Performs a binary safe case-insensitive string comparison

string strchr(string haystack, string needle) *3.0*

An alias for `strstr()`

int strcmp(string str1, string str2) *3.0*

Performs a binary safe string comparison

int strcoll(string str1, string str2) *4.0.5*

Compares two strings using the current locale

int strcspn(string str, string mask) *3.0.3*

Finds length of initial segment consisting entirely of characters not found in `mask`

resource stream_context_create([array options]) *4.3.0*

Creates a file context and optionally sets parameters

array stream_context_get_options(resource context|resource stream) *4.3.0*

Retrieves options for a stream/wrapper/context

bool stream_context_set_option(resource context|resource stream, string wrappername, string optionname, mixed value) *4.3.0*

Sets an option for a wrapper

bool stream_context_set_params(resource context|resource stream, array options) *4.3.0*
Sets parameters for a file context

string strftime(string format[, int timestamp]) *3.0*
Formats a local time/date according to locale settings

string strip_tags(string str[, string allowable_tags]) *3.0.8*
Strips HTML and PHP tags from a string

string stripcslashes(string str) *4.0*
Strips backslashes from a string; uses C-style conventions

string stripslashes(string str) *3.0*
Strips backslashes from a string

string stristr(string haystack, string needle) *3.0.6*
Finds first occurrence of a string within another (case-insensitive)

int strlen(string str) *3.0*
Gets string length

int strnatcasecmp(string s1, string s2) *4.0*
Returns the result of case-insensitive string comparison using natural algorithm

int strnatcmp(string s1, string s2) *4.0*
Returns the result of string comparison using natural algorithm

int strncasecmp(string str1, string str2, int len) *4.0.2*
Performs a binary safe string comparison of len characters

int strncmp(string str1, string str2, int len) *4.0*
Performs a binary safe string comparison of len characters

int strpos(string haystack, string needle[, int offset]) *3.0*
Finds position of first occurrence of a string within another

string strrchr(string haystack, string needle) *3.0*
Finds the last occurrence of a character in a string within another

string strrev(string str) *3.0*
Reverses a string

int strrpos(string haystack, string needle)   3.0
    Finds position of last occurrence of a character in a string within another

int strspn(string str, string mask)   3.0.3
    Finds length of initial segment consisting entirely of characters found in `mask`

string strstr(string haystack, string needle)   3.0
    Finds first occurrence of a string within another

string strtok([string str,] string token)   3.0
    Tokenizes a string

string strtolower(string str)   3.0
    Makes a string lowercase

int strtotime(string time, int now)   3.0.12
    Converts string representation of date and time to a timestamp

string strtoupper(string str)   3.0
    Makes a string uppercase

string strtr(string str, string from, string to)   3.0
    Translates characters in `str` using given translation tables

string strval(mixed var)   3.0
    Gets the string value of a variable

string substr(string str, int start[, int length])   3.0
    Returns part of a string

int substr_count(string haystack, string needle)   4.0
    Returns the number of times a substring occurs in the string

string substr_replace(string str, string repl, int start[, int length])   4.0
    Replaces part of a string with another string

switch(expr)   3.0
    Language keyword that implements the C-like `switch` construct

int symlink(string target, string link)   3.0
    Creates a symbolic link

bool syslog(int priority, string message)   3.0
    Generates a system log message

int system(string command[, int return_value]) *3.0*
    Executes an external program and displays output

float tan(float number) *3.0*
    Returns the tangent of the number in radians

float tanh(float number) *4.1.0*
    Returns the hyperbolic tangent of the number

string tempnam(string dir, string prefix) *3.0*
    Creates a unique filename in a directory

string textdomain(string domain) *3.0.7*
    Sets the textdomain to domain; returns the current domain

int time(void) *3.0*
    Returns current Unix timestamp

resource tmpfile(void) *3.0.13*
    Creates a temporary file that will be deleted automatically after use

bool touch(string filename[, int time[, int atime]]) *3.0*
    Sets modification time of file

void trigger_error(string messsage[, int error_type]) *4.0.1*
    Generates a user-level error/warning/notice message

string trim(string str[, string character_mask]) *3.0*
    Strips whitespace from the beginning and end of a string

bool uasort(array array_arg, string cmp_function) *3.0.4*
    Sorts an array with a user-defined comparison function and maintains index association

string ucfirst(string str) *3.0*
    Makes a string's first character uppercase

string ucwords(string str) *3.0.3*
    Uppercases the first character of every word in a string

bool uksort(array array_arg, string cmp_function) *3.0.4*
    Sorts an array by keys using a user-defined comparison function

int umask([int mask]) *3.0*
    Returns or changes the umask

string uniqid(string prefix[, bool more_entropy])   *3.0*
    Generates a unique ID

int unixtojd([int timestamp])   *4.0*
    Converts Unix timestamp to Julian day count

bool unlink(string filename)   *3.0*
    Deletes a file

array unpack(string format, string input)   *3.0*
    Unpacks binary string into named array elements according to format argument

void unregister_tick_function(string function_name)   *4.0.3*
    Unregisters a tick callback function

mixed unserialize(string variable_representation)   *3.0.5*
    Takes a string representation of variable and recreates it

void unset(mixed var[, mixed var[, ...]])   *3.0*
    Unsets a given variable

string urldecode(string str)   *3.0*
    Decodes URL-encoded string

string urlencode(string str)   *3.0*
    URL-encodes a string

void usleep(int micro_seconds)   *3.0*
    Delays for a given number of microseconds

bool usort(array array_arg, string cmp_function)   *3.0.3*
    Sorts an array by values using a user-defined comparison function

string utf8_decode(string data)   *3.0.6*
    Converts a UTF-8 encoded string to ISO-8859-1

string utf8_encode(string data)   *3.0.6*
    Encodes an ISO-8859-1 string to UTF-8

var $prop   *3.0*
    Language keyword that defines a property in a class

void var_dump(mixed var)   *3.0.5*
    Dumps a string representation of a variable to output

---

mixed var_export(mixed var[, bool return]) *4.1.0*
    Outputs or returns a string representation of a variable

int version_compare(string ver1, string ver2[, string oper]) *4.1.0*
    Compares two PHP-standardized version number strings

bool virtual(string filename) *3.0*
    Performs an Apache subrequest

int vprintf(string format, array args) *4.1.0*
    Outputs a formatted string

string vsprintf(string format, array args) *4.1.0*
    Returns a formatted string

while(cond) *3.0*
    Language keyword that implements a loop that continues until cond is false

string wordwrap(string str[, int width[, string break[, int cut]]]) *4.0.2*
    Wraps buffer to selected number of characters using string break character

string xml_error_string(int code) *3.0.6*
    Gets XML parser error string

int xml_get_current_byte_index(resource parser) *3.0.6*
    Gets current byte index for an XML parser

int xml_get_current_column_number(resource parser) *3.0.6*
    Gets current column number for an XML parser

int xml_get_current_line_number(resource parser) *3.0.6*
    Gets current line number for an XML parser

int xml_get_error_code(resource parser) *3.0.6*
    Gets XML parser error code

int xml_parse(resource parser, string data[, int isFinal]) *3.0.6*
    Starts parsing an XML document

int xml_parse_into_struct(resource parser, string data, array &struct, array &index) *3.0.8*
    Parses a XML document

resource xml_parser_create([string encoding]) *3.0.6*
    Creates an XML parser

resource xml_parser_create_ns([string encoding[, string sep]])   *4.0.5*
    Creates an XML parser

int xml_parser_free(resource parser)   *3.0.6*
    Frees an XML parser

int xml_parser_get_option(resource parser, int option)   *3.0.6*
    Gets options from an XML parser

int xml_parser_set_option(resource parser, int option, mixed value)   *3.0.6*
    Sets options in an XML parser

int xml_set_character_data_handler(resource parser, string hdl)   *3.0.6*
    Sets up character data handler

int xml_set_default_handler(resource parser, string hdl)   *3.0.6*
    Sets up default handler

int xml_set_element_handler(resource parser, string shdl, string ehdl)   *3.0.6*
    Sets up start and end element handlers

int xml_set_end_namespace_decl_handler(resource parser, string hdl)   *4.0.5*
    Sets up character data handler

int xml_set_external_entity_ref_handler(resource parser, string hdl)   *3.0.6*
    Sets up external entity reference handler

int xml_set_notation_decl_handler(resource parser, string hdl)   *3.0.6*
    Sets up notation declaration handler

int xml_set_object(resource parser, object &obj)   *4.0*
    Sets up object that should be used for callbacks

int xml_set_processing_instruction_handler(resource parser, string hdl)   *3.0.6*
    Sets up processing instruction (PI) handler

int xml_set_start_namespace_decl_handler(resource parser, string hdl)   *4.0.5*
    Sets up character data handler

int xml_set_unparsed_entity_decl_handler(resource parser, string hdl)   *3.0.6*
    Sets up unparsed entity declaration handler

XOR   *3.0*
    Language keyword that is similar to the ^ operator, except lower precedence

resource xslt_create(void)   *4.0.3*
    Creates a new XSLT processor

---

int xslt_errno(resource processor)   *4.0.3*
    Returns an error number

string xslt_error(resource processor)   *4.0.3*
    Returns an error string

void xslt_free(resource processor)   *4.0.3*
    Frees the XSLT processor

string xslt_process(resource processor, string xml, string xslt[,
mixed result[, array args[, array params]]]])   *4.0.3*
    Performs the XSLT transformation

void xslt_set_base(resource processor, string base)   *4.0.5*
    Sets the base URI for all XSLT transformations

void xslt_set_encoding(resource processor, string encoding)   *4.0.5*
    Sets the output encoding for the current stylesheet

void xslt_set_error_handler(resource processor, mixed error_func)   *4.0.4*
    Sets the error handler to be called when an XSLT error occurs

void xslt_set_log(resource processor, string logfile)   *4.0.6*
    Sets the log file to write the errors to (defaults to *stderr*)

void xslt_set_sax_handlers(resource processor, array handlers)   *4.0.6*
    Sets the SAX handlers to be called when the XML document
    gets processed

void xslt_set_scheme_handlers(resource processor, array handlers)   *4.0.6*
    Sets the scheme handlers for the XSLT processor

string zend_version(void)   *4.0*
    Get the version of the Zend Engine

void zip_close(resource zip)   *4.1.0*
    Closes a ZIP archive

void zip_entry_close(resource zip_ent)   *4.1.0*
    Closes a ZIP entry

int zip_entry_compressedsize(resource zip_entry)   *4.1.0*
    Returns the compressed size of a ZIP entry

string zip_entry_compressionmethod(resource zip_entry)   *4.1.0*
    Returns a string containing the compression method used on
    a particular entry

int zip_entry_filesize(resource zip_entry)   *4.1.0*
     Returns the actual file size of a ZIP entry

string zip_entry_name(resource zip_entry)   *4.1.0*
     Returns the name given a ZIP entry

bool zip_entry_open(resource zip_dp, resource zip_entry, string mode)   *4.1.0*
     Opens the ZIP file pointed to by the resource entry

string zip_entry_read(resource zip_ent[, int length])   *4.1.0*
     Reads bytes from an opened ZIP entry

resource zip_open(string filename)   *4.1.0*
     Opens a new ZIP archive for reading

resource zip_read(resource zip)   *4.1.0*
     Returns the next file in the archive

Related Titles Available from O'Reilly

Web Programming

ActionScript Cookbook

ActionScript for Flash MX
Pocket Reference

ActionScript for Flash MX:
The Definitive Guide,
2nd Edition

Creating Applications
with Mozilla

Dynamic HTML: The Definitive Reference, *2nd Edition*

Flash Remoting:
The Definitive Guide

Google Hacks

Google Pocket Guide

HTTP: The Definitive Guide

JavaScript & DHTML Cookbook

JavaScript Pocket Reference,
2nd Edition

JavaScript: The Definitive Guide,
4th Edition

PHP 5 Essentials

PHP Cookbook

Programming ColdFusion MX,
2nd Edition

Programming PHP

Web Database Applications
with PHP and MySQL,
2nd Edition

Webmaster in a Nutshell,
3rd Edition

Cascading Style Sheets:
The Definitive Guide,
2nd Edition

CSS Pocket Reference

Dreamweaver MX 2004:
The Missing Manual

HTML & XHTML:
The Definitive Guide,
5th Edition

HTML Pocket Reference,
2nd Edition

Information Architecture
for the World Wide Web,
2nd Edition

Learning Web Design,
2nd Edition

Web Design in a Nutshell,
2nd Edition

Web Administration

Apache Cookbook

Apache Pocket Reference

Apache: The Definitive Guide,
3rd Edition

Essential Blogging

Perl for Web Site Management

Squid: The Definitive Guide

Web Performance Tuning,
2nd Edition

Web Authoring and Design

O'REILLY®

Keep in touch with O'Reilly

1. Download examples from our books

To find example files for a book, go to:
www.oreilly.com/catalog
select the book, and follow the "Examples" link.

2. Register your O'Reilly books

Register your book at *register.oreilly.com*

Why register your books? Once you've registered your O'Reilly books you can:

- Win O'Reilly books, T-shirts or discount coupons in our monthly drawing.
- Get special offers available only to registered O'Reilly customers.
- Get catalogs announcing new books (US and UK only).
- Get email notification of new editions of the O'Reilly books you own.

3. Join our email lists

Sign up to get topic-specific email announcements of new books and conferences, special offers, and O'Reilly Network technology newsletters at:
elists.oreilly.com

It's easy to customize your free elists subscription so you'll get exactly the O'Reilly news you want.

4. Get the latest news, tips, and tools
www.oreilly.com

- "Top 100 Sites on the Web"—PC Magazine
- CIO Magazine's Web Business 50 Awards

Our web site contains a library of comprehensive product information (including book excerpts and tables of contents), downloadable software, background articles, interviews with technology leaders, links to relevant sites, book cover art, and more.

5. Work for O'Reilly

Check out our web site for current employment opportunities:
jobs.oreilly.com

6. Contact us

O'Reilly & Associates
1005 Gravenstein Hwy North
Sebastopol, CA 95472 USA

TEL: 707-827-7000 or 800-998-9938
        (6am to 5pm PST)

FAX: 707-829-0104

order@oreilly.com
> For answers to problems regarding your order or our products.
> To place a book order online, visit:
> *www.oreilly.com/order_new*

catalog@oreilly.com
> To request a copy of our latest catalog.

booktech@oreilly.com
> For book content technical questions or corrections.

corporate@oreilly.com
> For educational, library, government, and corporate sales.

proposals@oreilly.com
> To submit new book proposals to our editors and product managers.

international@oreilly.com
> For information about our international distributors or translation queries. For a list of our distributors outside of North America check out:
> *international.oreilly.com/distributors.html*

adoption@oreilly.com
> For information about academic use of O'Reilly books, visit:
> *academic.oreilly.com*

O'REILLY®

Our books are available at most retail and online bookstores.
To order direct: 1-800-998-9938 • *order@oreilly.com* • *www.oreilly.com*
Online editions of most O'Reilly titles are available at *safari.oreilly.com*